HOW TO MAKE CLOTHES THAT FIT AND FLATTER

Books by Adele P. Margolis

HOW TO MAKE CLOTHES THAT FIT AND FLATTER
THE DRESSMAKING BOOK
PATTERN WISE
THE COMPLETE BOOK OF TAILORING
HOW TO DESIGN YOUR OWN DRESS PATTERNS

HOW TO MAKE CLOTHES THAT FIT AND FLATTER

❖❖❖❖❖

ADELE P. MARGOLIS

DOUBLEDAY & COMPANY, INC.
GARDEN CITY, NEW YORK

To all my very dear friends
        (they know who they are)
who have believed in me, supported me in crisis,
cheered me in success, and surrounded me with their love.

CONTENTS

tern—how to use the basic pattern with a style pattern: simple pattern comparisons, more complex pattern comparisons—the dress form, another you—how to make a dressmaker's dummy: the French-lining cover, how to fit the cover, how and with what to pad the form—a sleeve form—a papier-mâché form: what materials you need to make it, how to apply the tapes, how to finish the form —fitting that you can do for yourself and how: places you can reach, places you can't reach and what to do about them

INTRODUCTION

You would think that after wearing clothes for years, one would know a dress that fits from one that doesn't. Unfortunately, this is not so. Most women wear clothes with a "near'ems" sort of fit.

Take the gal dependent on ready-to-wear. Lured by the design, urged on by a saleslady anxious to sell what's at hand, jammed into a fitting room often too small to see herself adequately, desperately in need of a dress right this very minute, she squeezes herself into the nearest promising little number. If she can zip it over her hips, it's a sale. Never mind the darts, the shaping seams, the ease. Everyone will be so dazzled by the design and the prestigious name of the designer that no one will even notice its bad fit. Besides, her friends buy in exactly the same way. They can't afford to be critical.

The truth is that the woman who buys her clothes must accept this kind of fit or go in for alterations frequently extensive and always expensive. Often, even when aware that something is wrong, neither the customer, the saleslady, nor the fitter (Alas!) knows just what is wrong or what can be done about it.

For those who have the time, patience, and money, custom-made clothes may well be the answer to faultless fit. The only problem is to find a dressmaker or tailor who can fit as well as sew. Many professionals whose workmanship leaves nothing to be desired flunk out completely when it comes to fitting. Then, too, for an impatient generation accustomed to speed in everything and that wants what it wants when it wants it, construction seems irritatingly slow and fittings much too time consuming.

Well, there's home sewing as the way of dealing with the problem at a price one can afford and a tempo one can more or less control.

That's the ideal, anyway. How to achieve it is another matter—the most vexing in home sewing. More homemade clothing looks that way because of poor fit than because of poor workmanship. Many home sewers are extremely competent sewers—even talented ones. More are discouraged by their inability to fit than by their inability to master the techniques of dressmaking or tailoring.

There is not a one of us who sews who does not long for some gimmick, some gadget, some sure-fire formula for success in fitting. Alas, there is none!

Fitting is an art and part of an art—that of creating beautiful clothes. As with other arts, it takes time, thought, and practice. Any complex subject becomes understandable through study. That's about the best one can offer by way of an "easy" solution of fitting problems. If you know how and where a garment should fit, that's half the battle. If you know what to do about it when it doesn't, that's the other half. Armed with this information, every sewer can learn to be a good fitter.

Philadelphia, Pennsylvania
November, 1967   ADELE POLLOCK MARGOLIS

HOW TO MAKE
CLOTHES
THAT FIT
AND FLATTER

Chapter I

THE FIGURE OF FASHION

HOW TO CHOOSE THE RIGHT SIZE, THE RIGHT FIGURE TYPE, THE RIGHT FOUNDATION

One may as well face it at the start. You only get out of a fashion what you put into it by way of a figure!

Fifty years ago, the fashionable American woman was size 16 going on size 18. Today she is size 12 going on size 10. Tables of statistics have made her health conscious. Mass media have made her youth conscious. Size has become a status symbol.

At the moment, the ideal figure is young, younger, youngest—a cruel blow to those beyond the first flush of youth. As long as the world continues to be swamped with young people (more than half the world's present population is under thirty with percentages increasing steadily in their favor) and as long as the great portion of the earned, accumulated, and inherited buying power is in their hands, just so long will the fashion industry (among others) continue to design and produce for youth.

Fair or unfair, if you wish to look fashionable today, you must strive for a slender, youthful figure even if you are no longer young. The "stylish stouts" went out of fashion a long time ago.

Fashion Comes in Sizes

The Giant Size Is Not the Economy Size. If you're size 16 or over, you're out of luck. Some stores don't even stock anything over a 14. Clothing buyers and store managers tell us that the best-selling sizes across the country today are the 10's and 12's. The largest choices and the best buys are in these smaller sizes.

There's no doubt about it! Slim figures *are* easier to dress. What figure faults they possess (and they do!) can more easily be hidden. What on earth can hide a bulge or a roll of fat except a "tent" dress or some variation of a maternity dress? Many a fitting problem would diminish with the loss of a few pounds and a little exercise. But not all! A weight loss alone will not solve fitting problems attributable to build or age. Were I, for example, to lose the twenty pounds that would bring me back to the skinny days of my youth, the problem of sloping shoulders, a pyramidal structure, a thickening waistline, and a sagging bosom would still plague me. *But* I would have a wider selection of styles available to me and with some adjustment they would look vastly better on me.

If twenty pounds is an out-of-the-question weight loss for one who has lived enough years to consider her evening cocktail and a gourmet meal among the finer things in life, then at least one can think thin and try for ten. In the ensuing struggle, it's a comfort to know that *it is better to fit the clothes you would like to wear than to make the clothes fit what you are*—especially if what you are is anything less than great.

What's Standard?

Simply because it is the only practical way to deal with the problem of size for the millions of buyers of both ready-to-wear clothes and of patterns, these must be sold in standard sizes. In recent years, in a valiant effort to accommodate variations among women, patterns and clothes have been cut for figure types as well. There is now on the market a whole array of designs for misses, women, half-sizes, talls, shorts, full-bosomed, flat-chested, long-waisted, juniors, junior-petites, young junior/teens. The hope is that choosing the proper size and figure type will guarantee clothes that really fit.

Sad to say, even those whose measurements are within the ranges of the so-called "standard" for size and type may depart from it in some little ways. Figures are no more alike than thumbprints. All of the gals in Fig. 1 take the same size yet their figures are not the same. Were they to turn around and face you, the differences would be even more striking. About all that the designation size 10 or 20 or

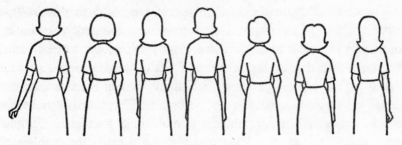

Fig. 1

40 really means is that it is THE size that most nearly coincides with a person's measurements.

Many women think that when they hit on the right size good fit automatically will follow. This is a reasonable expectation. Yet, size is only part of the picture. The shaping of a garment in relation to the body beneath is of the utmost importance. A standard degree of shaping is, of course, implied in a standard size. The truth of the matter is that practically no one is a perfect standard size. Some who claim they are may not know what constitutes good fit. Others may know but be willing to settle for less-than-perfect fit.

Even assuming one were a perfect size, how can one be sure the garment was cut accurately or that it was stitched along the designated lines. In any production—assembly line or individual—it is fair to suppose a degree of human error.

To add to the confusion, one cannot assume that a ready-to-wear size is the size one should choose for a pattern. It is too variable. A size is anything a particular manufacturer and his staff decide it is from their experience. The clothing industry has never adopted a uniform system of sizing. Who can blame them? A manufacturer who makes his fortune on a unique set of measurements is hardly inclined to share the secrets of his success with his competitors. Americans are great brand-name buyers. If Mr. X's skirt or dress or suit fits to a fare-thee-well, naturally one will always look for a garment that bears his label.

The "easy" look of current fashion has been a boon to manufacturer and consumer alike. Many styles might just as well be (some actually are) designed for small, medium, and large. Their unfitted lines cover a multitude of figure problems. Many of those who at first stubbornly resisted the skimmer dress have been completely won over not only by its comfort but more importantly its problem-free fit. Some even view with dismay the return of fitted clothing.

It is an interesting paradox that many women who are happy enough buying smaller sizes in ready-to-wear will anxiously buy larger sizes in patterns. Their fearfulness is quite understandable. Cutting does, indeed, seem so final. They reason that it is easy enough to make a garment smaller but how can you add once the cloth is cut?

The truth of the matter is that it can be quite as impossible to fit something cut too large as too small. For many figures, the part of the garment most difficult to fit is apt to be narrow—the neck-shoulder-chest area. Excess fabric complicates the fitting of neckline, collar, shoulders, and sleeves. Often, too, style lines are irretrievably thrown off. It may take a little experimenting but it is extremely important that home sewers determine *the* size easiest for them to work with.

Just as ready-to-wear offers a range of fashions for various figure types, so does the pattern industry. What one must realize in both instances is that not every style is available in every size. What may look smashing on a junior size figure may look lamentable on a half-size, though both are designed for figures that require shortened bodice lengths.

Determine Your Figure Type

You may know your figure type from your buying experience. If

miss-woman junior   half-size   teen   sub-teen junior petite.chubbie   girl

Fig. 2

you are not certain, consult the measurements chart. The widest selection of patterns and styles is in the misses and women's styles. If you are another figure type, you may, when you learn to work with patterns, be able to choose any pattern and adjust it to your needs.

How to Select Your Pattern Size

Wouldn't it be great if you could try on a pattern for size as you can a dress when you buy it?

You must try the dress on! As we have seen from the foregoing discussion, size is what a manufacturer says it is. However, once you've worked out your correct size in a commercial pattern you can depend on a certain uniformity whatever the pattern company and whether the pattern be for dress, coat, or suit.

All patterns are created from a "staple" (sometimes called a block, master, or basic pattern) made to body measurements plus ease. In commercial patterns these are drafted from a set of standard measurements approved and adopted by the Measurement Standard Committee of the Pattern Industry. See page 6. Patterns created by the Spadea Company are the exception to this. See page 7.

To Determine Your Size, Take a Few Measurements and Compare Them with the Standard Measurement Chart. The best measurements are taken over a slip rather than over your dress. Wear the foundation garments you generally wear or those you plan to wear with the garment you are making.

Using a non-stretch tape measure, measure your bust around the fullest part. This is a snug but not tight measurement. Measure your waist comfortably. For a skirt or pants, measure the waist while seated. Measure your hips around the fullest part.

You'll need some help for the next measurement. Tie a string around your waist to define it. Bend your head forward. Locate the prominent bone at which your head is hinged. Straighten up. Have someone measure the distance between this socket bone and the waistline string.

These four measurements—bust, waist, hips, and center-back length—are the ones used for comparison with the standards listed in the measurement charts.

Measurement Chart for all Pattern Companies

COMPARISON OF BODY MEASUREMENT CHARTS

Approved by the Measurement Standard Committee of the Pattern Fashion Industry
Butterick, McCall's, Simplicity, Vogue

MISSES'

Size	6	8	10	12	14	16	18
Bust	30½	31½	32½	34	36	38	40
Waist	22	23	24	25½	27	29	31
Hip	32½	33½	34½	36	38	40	42
Back Waist Length	15½	15¾	16	16¼	16½	16¾	17

WOMEN'S

Size	38	40	42	44	46	48	50
Bust	42	44	46	48	50	52	54
Waist	34	36	38	40½	43	45½	48
Hip	44	46	48	50	52	54	56
Back Waist Length	17¼	17⅜	17½	17⅝	17¾	17⅞	18

HALF-SIZE

Size	10½	12½	14½	16½	18½	20½	22½	24½
Bust	33	35	37	39	41	43	45	47
Waist	26	28	30	32	34	36½	39	41½
Hip	35	37	39	41	43	45½	48	50½
Back Waist Length	15	15¼	15½	15¾	15⅞	16	16⅛	16¼

JUNIOR PETITE

Size	3	5	7	9	11	13
Bust	30½	31	32	33	34	35
Waist	22	22½	23½	24½	25½	26½
Hip	31½	32	33	34	35	36
Back Waist Length	14	14¼	14½	14¾	15	15¼

JUNIOR

Size	5	7	9	11	13	15
Bust	30	31	32	33½	35	37
Waist	21½	22½	23½	24½	26	28
Hip	32	33	34	35½	37	39
Back Waist Length	15	15¼	15½	15¾	16	16¼

YOUNG JUNIOR/TEEN

Size	5/6	7/8	9/10	11/12	13/14	15/16
Bust	28	29	30½	32	33½	35
Waist	22	23	24	25	26	27
Hip	31	32	33½	35	36½	38
Back Waist Length	13½	14	14½	15	15⅜	15¾

GIRLS

Size	7	8	10	12	14
Breast	26	27	28½	30	32
Waist	23	23½	24½	25½	26½
Hip	27	28	30	32	34
Back Waist Length	11½	12	12¾	13½	14¼

Spadea's Ready-to-wear Size Charts

Regular sizing

Sizes	6	8	10	12	14	16	18	20
Bust	32	33	34	35	36½	38	40	42
Waist	22	23	24	25	26½	28	30	32
Hip (5" below waistline)	33	34	35	36	37½	39	41	43
Length (nape of neck to waist)	16	16¼	16½	16¾	17	17¼	17½	17¾

For mature figures

Sizes	14	16	18	20	40	42	44
Bust	36½	38	40	42	44	46	48
Waist	27½	29	31	33	35	37	38
Hip (5″ below waistline)	37½	39	41	43	45	47	49
Length (nape of neck to waist)	17	17¼	17½	17¾	18	18¼	18½

For diminutives (short figures, 5′5″ and under)

Sizes	8	10	12	14	16	18	20
Bust	33	34	35	36½	38	40	42
Waist	24	25	26	27½	29	31	33
Hip (5″ below waistline)	34	35	36	37½	39	41	43
Length (nape of neck to waist)	15¾	16	16¼	16½	16¾	17	17¼

For tall girls

Sizes	8	10	12	14	16	18	20
Bust	33	34	35	36½	38	40	42
Waist	23	24	25	26½	28	30	32
Hip (5″ below waistline)	34	35	36	37½	39	41	43
Length (nape of neck to waist)	17	17¼	17½	17¾	18	18¼	18½

For half-sizes

Sizes	12½	14½	16½	18½	20½	22½
Bust	35½	37½	39½	41½	43½	45½
Waist	27½	29½	31½	33½	35½	37½
Hip (5″ below waistline)	35½	37½	39½	41½	43½	45½
Length (nape of neck to waist)	15¾	16	16¼	16½	16¾	17

For junior sizes

Sizes	5	7	9	11	13	15	17
Bust	31½	32½	33½	34½	36	37½	39
Waist	21½	22½	23½	24½	26	27½	29
Hip (5″ below waistline)	32½	33½	34½	35½	37	38½	40
Length (nape of neck to waist)	15½	15¾	16	16¼	16½	16¾	17

Coats (capes, stoles, aprons)

Sizes	Small	Medium	Large
Bust	33–34	35–36½	38–40
Waist (used if garment has waistline)	23–24	25–26½	28–30
Hip (5″ below waistline)	34–35	36–37½	39–41

These charts are also to be found in all complete pattern catalogues.

Read through the chart until you locate a set of measurements most nearly like your own. If you are a rarity, you may match all four measurements. If you are lucky, perhaps three of the four. If you are a borderline size, that is, somewhere between two sizes, choose the smaller size and grade it up. (It is generally easier to make a pattern larger than smaller.) Should the discrepancy between bodice and skirt be very great—say, a difference of more than one size—it may be advisable to buy two patterns, one for the bodice and another for the skirt, altering both so they join at the waistline. This would be particularly desirable if the design had considerable detail.

Since the bodice is most difficult to fit, size is usually determined by the bust measurement. In simple patterns, waist and hips are comparatively easy to adjust. A method for choosing pattern size advocated by experienced pattern saleswomen is as follows: If you are 5 foot 5 inches or under, choose a pattern one size smaller than your bust measurement would indicate; if you are tall or large-bosomed, choose the size indicated by the bust measurement. Take into account your shoulder width. If you are broad-shouldered or square-shouldered, use the size indicated. If you are narrow-shouldered you may be able to get away with a smaller size.

The style of the garment may also be a determining factor in the choice of size. If the design has much fullness, you may be able to wear a smaller size. If it is very fitted, you may need a larger size.

Choose the same size for suits and coats as for dresses. All the necessary additional allowances have already been made in the pattern.

There are probably as many theories and tricks about selecting the correct pattern size as there are people working in this field. Unfortunately, there is no sure way. So many figures defy all the rules. The sewer herself must decide the size that best suits her with the least amount of adjustment. This can only come from experimentation.

Take It Easy!

You cannot fit a dress as if it were a second skin. In the first place, most of us don't have the kind of figures that can take it. Secondly, most fabrics don't have sufficient "give" to permit body movement if fitted tightly.

Clothes must have a little more room—room to make them comfortable and room to conceal figure imperfections. This additional room is called *ease*. All garments have it in varying amounts. How much depends on

1. *the function of the garment*
   You need a lot more ease in sportswear than you do in a cocktail dress. After all, how much movement does it take to lift a martini?

2. *the design of the garment*
   Some styles have much more fullness than others. The designer decides this.

3. *your personal preference*
   Some feel self-conscious in a tight-fitting dress and others aren't happy unless their clothes fit like a flamenco dancer's.

It is difficult and often unwise to give standard amounts of ease. An amount that's right for one person may be altogether wrong for another. If you just want to stand around decoratively, you'll need less ease. If you're the type that insists on moving around, you'll want more. If you're heavy, you'll need more; your muscles in motion take up more room. If you're an active type, you'll feel imprisoned by a dress that encases you. An uncomfortably snug dress that keeps you tugging at it may spoil your fun and your looks. A comfortable one leaves you free to enjoy all around you without worrying about "bustin' out all over"—like June.

Having said all that—here are suggested *minimum* amounts for a fitted dress for those who must have some rule of thumb to go by: bust—3 inches, waist—0 to ½ inches, hips—2 inches, across the chest—½ inch, across the back—½ inch, biceps—2 inches, bodice length—½ inch, sleeve length—enough so it does not ride up when the arm is bent. A fitted suit has an inch more ease through the bust and waist than a dress. A fitted coat—two extra inches in these places. The sleeves of both coats and suits are proportionately fuller to fit the enlarged armholes.

Here is one way to tell how much ease you like in your clothes. Try on a favorite dress (or suit or coat). Pinch out the excess fabric until the garment fits tight against the body. Measure the amount of fabric in the "pinch." This ease is added to your body measurements. The total is then compared with the measurements of the pattern. *The pattern you buy has the ease built right into it. You do not need to add any.* However, you may find that you want a little more or less ease than the pattern provides. If so, you can add or subtract the amount you choose. See page 95 for directions.

While most pattern companies start with the same basic body measurements, they have different policies in regard to ease. Some add more, some less. (All of them add more than the minimum amounts indicated above.) Most often, the amount of ease is determined by the designer. All of these things make the amount of ease in a pattern an unpredictable quantity.

The difference in the amounts of ease added to body measurements accounts for the differences in the fit of patterns produced by

the various companies. This may explain why you prefer one above
the others.

Grading

Sewing is a great deal simpler when working with a pattern in *the*
right size. However, there are times when one wishes she knew how
to make a desirable pattern a size larger or smaller. This is particularly true for women with very tiny or very large figures who find that
the most appealing patterns are not to be found in their sizes.

*Grading is the process of increasing or decreasing a pattern from
one size to the next.* The change is *gradual* rather than in one place
(Fig. 3), hence the term "grading."

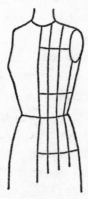

Fig. 3

Grading is also *proportionate* rather than uniform. This is because,
in growth, the bony structure of the body does not increase in the
same amounts as the fleshy parts. Therefore there is less differential
in bony areas than in fleshy areas as patterns are graded from one
size to another. Fig. 4 suggests a generally acceptable amount and
placement of grades for misses and women's sizes.

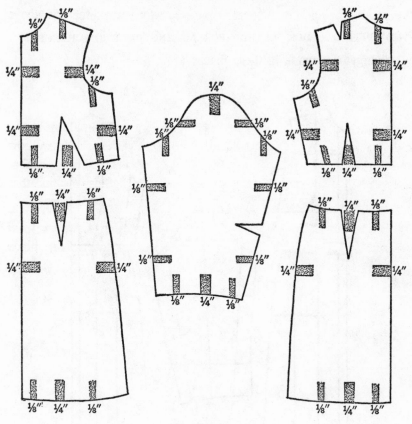

Fig. 4

In industry, grading is now generally done by computers. For the occasional needs of the home sewer the following methods work well. There are two: one is to split or tuck the pattern to make necessary changes (Fig. 6); the other is to shift the pattern pieces from one point to another (Fig. 7). Use whichever seems easier for you.

The grading directions given below are for the five pattern pieces which make up the basic pattern—bodice front and back, skirt front and back, and sleeve. It is not likely that your grading will be confined to anything quite so simple. You will have to decide how these overall amounts can be divided for the number of pieces in your pattern. Just remember that all pieces that join must have similar adjustments.

THE SPLIT OR TUCK METHOD FOR MAKING PATTERN CHANGES

Changes are made in these places (Fig. 5).

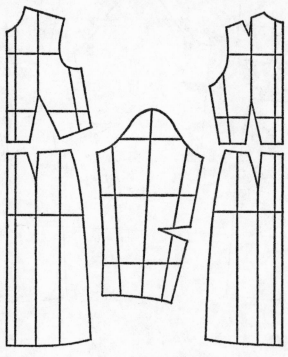

Fig. 5

TO MAKE THE PATTERN LARGER—slash and spread

1. Draw slash lines where indicated in Fig. 5. Slash the pattern along these lines.

2. Spread the pattern to the amounts suggested in Fig. 4. Fill in the open spaces with tissue (Fig. 6a).

TO MAKE THE PATTERN SMALLER—slash and overlap or tuck

1. Draw slash lines where indicated in Fig. 5.

2. Either slash the pattern along these lines and overlap to the

amount indicated in Fig. 4 OR fold along the slash lines and tuck the pattern to the designated amount (Fig. 6b).

3. Scotch tape to position.

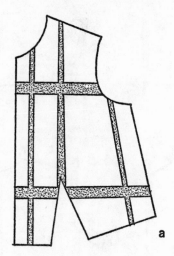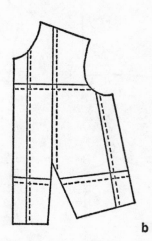

Fig. 6

THE SHIFTING METHOD

1. Draw a new center back line. Place the center back of the pattern along this line then shift it up ¼ inch from A to B. Trace the B corner (Fig. 7a).

2. Always keeping the center back of the pattern parallel to the new center back line, shift the pattern out ⅛ inch. Trace the neckline to C (Fig. 7b).

3. Once more, shift the pattern out ⅛ inch. Trace the shoulder to D (Fig. 7c).

4. Shift the pattern down ¼ inch to E (notch). Trace from D to E (Fig. 7d).

5. Shift the pattern out ⅛ inch. Trace the armhole from E to F (Fig. 7e).

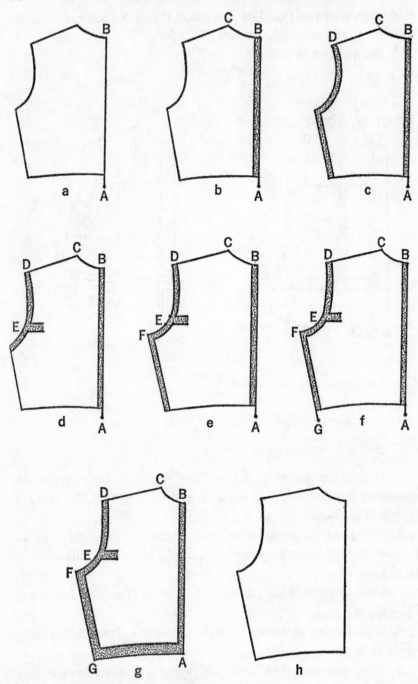

Fig. 7

6. Shift the pattern down ¼ inch to G. Trace the corner at G (Fig. 7f).

7. Shift the pattern down ½ inch and trace the waistline from G to A (Fig. 7g). This completes the grade (Fig. 7h).

To make a pattern smaller by this method shift the pattern back rather than out in the same amount.

Grade each of the pattern pieces in the same way. This is a faster method than the slash and spread or split and tuck method though the latter may be a little easier and more accurate for inexperienced graders.

"How Firm a Foundation"

There's absolutely no mystery about it any more! Those old-time unmentionables are today's common knowledge—thanks to present-day advertising. And small wonder—they're so photogenic! So attractive and so comfortable are they also that there really is no excuse for anyone no longer very young or very slender for not wearing what she needs to show off her clothes to best advantage.

Styles and silhouettes may change through the years but it's that familiar, female form with which designers have to cope. When you get right down to the bottom of things, it's the foundation garments that transform that same old shape into the figure of fashion. In the couture houses even the slenderest of mannequins may be required to wear that foundation garment which provides the figure lines essential to the design lines of the piece she is modeling. So important is this that if the appropriate underfashion isn't available, the couturier himself may create one especially suited to his designs.

American foundation garments are considered to be the finest in the world. Working closely with the fashion industry, manufacturers of brassieres and girdles are quick to provide the new figure lines demanded by the new fashions. The volume of advertising is so great in this field (look at any women's magazine) that it seems virtually impossible not to get the message that there is a garment for every size, type, function, and fashion. If this is not enough, good fitters are waiting in the wings in most department stores and specialty shops to individualize these standard garments to your requirements even further.

Each dress or suit that you make or buy requires a particular kind of control. Once you've determined what this should be for the garment in question, stick with it. A change in foundation garments will alter the fit. If you fit a bodice with one bra you may find all the darts and shaping seams in the wrong places if you substitute another in the wearing. If you fit a skirt with one girdle, you may find bulges or spanning if you substitute another in the wearing.

The fashionable figure is a trim one. From the standpoint of beauty, too, all bulges and rolls of fat are ugly. Get some professional advice on the type of garment that will "trim" you and the correct size to contain you.

"My Cup Runneth Over"

Should a tight bra presently in your possession cause your flesh to bulge above and below it, reposition the bra and redistribute the flesh to minimize the bulges.

Straps that dig into the shoulders are ugly as well as uncomfortable. Try substituting wide, padded lingerie straps. The new elastic straps are comfortable and better-looking but make heavy bosoms somewhat bouncy in motion.

Avoid bras that are too padded, too exaggerated, too rigid. Their appeal may be an obvious sexiness but true fashion achieves its allure in more subtle ways.

Transparent bras are sexy, too. But, if someone else does the fitting for you, spare her (or him) the embarrassment. Wear an opaque bra.

When there is bodice fullness, a normal length bra will do. For a fitted bodice with smooth diaphragm choose a long-line bra or an all-in-one. For a sleek, unbroken line, the all-in-one garment is best.

For evening wear, there is a great variety of strapless, backless, low-cut, and half bras. Needless to say, the decolletage and straps of a bra must conform to the decolletage of the dress.

Dresses with transparent tops call for strapless bras. Should a strapless bra not give you the support you need, try this: replace the bra straps with straps of flesh-colored illusion (a kind of tulle).

Heavily seamed or lace bras will show their raised surfaces under the following: very fitted dresses, knits, soft, lightweight, or smooth fabric. Find a bra of smooth fabric with as little seaming as possible.

A special bra built right into the dress guarantees the right lines. Dressmaker supply stores have bras of cotton or taffeta for this purpose. Or, you might want to sew into place one of your own just-right bras. Also available are foam rubber cups or foam rubber by the yard to be shaped as you desire. The latter is particularly good for providing a bosom line when the figure itself is flat.

Pull Yourself Together

When there is skirt fullness you can get away without a girdle. (This is one of the great appeals of dirndl-type skirts.) A straight skirt always requires a girdle.

For a sleek-unbroken line, an all-in-one garment is best. For general wear, the short girdles are sufficient. Panty-girdles, a must for pants and sportswear, are also popular for general wear.

Be sure to get a girdle that is long enough. It should fit vertically in length as well as horizontally in width. Short ones have a tendency to ride up.

Most of us spend more time sitting than standing. When selecting a girdle, try sitting in it so you may be sure of comfort along with control.

A too-tight girdle like a too-tight bra may cause bulges above and below it. Redistribute the flesh as directed for the bra. Better yet, get a larger size.

A girdle that fits the waist too tightly makes the stomach more prominent—that is if you can breathe long enough to see this.

Do REMEMBER: For a fitting always wear the undergarment you plan to wear with the garment.

It may be that some time in the future our ideas of beauty may change to the point when bras and girdles will no longer be desirable. As of now, however, no woman of fashion can afford to appear publicly without their shaping and support.

Chapter II

THE LOOK OF FASHION

HOW TO CREATE THE ILLUSION OF BEAUTY

A woman of fashion gives the illusion that she is dressed in an extraordinarily beautiful manner when in truth she may not have anything worthwhile on at all. She is a sort of feminine version of the Emperor's New Clothes.

Fashion deals in illusion—the illusion of beauty, of drama, of romance. The fashion-copy writers go on ecstatically about all this as anyone knows who watches television or reads the ads.

Contrary to the ancient epigram, seeing is deceiving! Scientists and psychologists tell us that the optical mechanism of the eyes may not see things as they really are, that the intellect does not always interpret the visual message correctly, and that our past experiences, imaginings, and even desires influence our interpretations. *"Trompe l'oeil"* has been the stock-in-trade of artists and artisans from earliest times.

Fashion creates its illusions with these elements of design—line, color, space, and texture. Since how the wearer appears to others is every bit as important as how she feels in her clothes, these very same art principles become primary considerations in the art of fitting.

Illusion by Design

LINE

Remember the old adage, "All roads lead to Rome"? To paraphrase this, all lines of a costume can lead to your most attractive feature. If you have a beautiful or arresting face, naturally you will want the lines to point this out. If your figure or your legs are notable, you will want all lines to focus on them. *The eye* obediently *follows the direction of a line*.

Fig. 8

In Fig. 8a, the eye is invited to continue indefinitely *in a vertical direction*. There is nothing to stop it. The resulting look is tall. (A dress with these lines may be fitted with considerable ease, if you wish, since the width of the garment is more than amply balanced by the unchecked vertical sweep of the eye movement.)

The eye may be instructed to move *in a specific direction*. In Fig. 8b, the eye is ordered to look up, making the head and shoulders the center of attention. In Fig. 8c, the eye is told to look down, making the figure the point of interest.

Eye movements may be stopped by setting limits. The width of the

picture hat and shoulder interest in Fig. 8d calls a halt to any vertical
eye movement. This sudden stop could make a short girl look even
shorter. The delimiting H lines of the front panel in Fig. 8e stop any
lateral eye movement, creating the illusion that the figure is only the
width of the panel.

When several lines appear as they do in most costumes, *the eye will
follow the most dominant one* (Fig. 9).

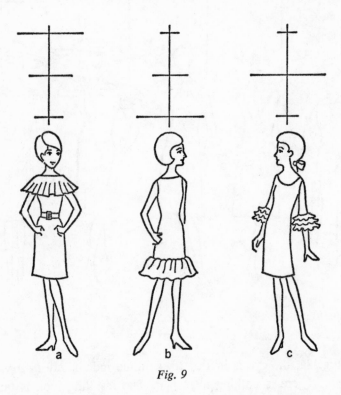

Fig. 9

In Fig. 9a, attention is focused on the shoulders and neckline.

In Fig. 9b, the eye is attracted to the flounce at the hemline.

In Fig. 9c, the eye is drawn to the bulk at the hipline.

If you have a lovely face, an attention-getting neckline and collar,
as in Fig. 9a, will frame it. If you have beautiful legs, a flirtatious
flounce, as in Fig. 9b, will invite the eye to linger on them. Only if
you have very slim hips can you dare sleeve ruffles that broaden the

hipline. Knowing that the eye will follow the dominant line in a design should make it possible for you to direct the eye wherever you wish.

In doing so be mindful of the fact that the eye is confused by contradictory lines (Fig. 10a) and too many lines, each vying for attention (Fig. 10b). The fussiness of both of these creates the illusion of size by inference. Somehow we cannot conceive of so much happening in so small a space. This is true of all cluttered areas.

a b c d

Fig. 10

When the lines of a costume pull in opposing directions—the upward curve of the hat, the downward curve of the cape in Fig. 10c—the eye is pulled in two directions. If the tension proves too great, one gives up looking; it's too much of a strain. The eye is pleased by a certain consistency. On the other hand, when the lines of a design are too much alike, the result is monotonous (Fig. 10d). One couldn't care less whether the wearer is small, large, or just right.

All of this hocus-pocus is pretty remarkable when you consider that there are only two kinds of lines that the designer can use to direct the eye to see what is or isn't there. A line can only be straight or curved. BUT, straight or curved, lines can be used on the vertical, the horizontal, the oblique. They can be short, long, or in between. Curved lines can also be subtle, slight, or deeply curved.

Straight vertical lines create the illusion of height, simplicity, dignity, stateliness (Fig. 11a). Straight horizontal lines suggest width, calmness, repose (Fig. 11b). Oblique lines lead the eye on. You expect them to go somewhere. They create the illusion of drama, movement (Fig. 11e). Downward curves make you feel sad (Fig. 11c); they droop. Upward curves give a lift (Fig. 11d); they make you feel gay. Combinations of curves create rhythm (Fig. 11f).

How Can All This Theory Be Applied to Your Choice of Style?

If you are tall and slender you can wear almost anything that will go with your coloring, your personality, and your activities. If you are short and slender, accentuate your petiteness. If you are anything other than these two, optical illusions for you.

If you are the tall, scrawny type, counteract the height with horizontal lines and details.

If you are the tall, heavy type, vertical lines will give the illusion of slenderness; horizontal lines will make you look shorter and heavier.

If you are short and deliciously (?) plump, vertical lines are the order of the day for you.

If you are narrow-shouldered and either big-bosomed or big-hipped, broaden the shoulder line to make the figure seem more in proportion.

If you are broad-shouldered and big-bosomed and short, avoid kimono-sleeved garments, particularly in suits and two-piece dresses. You'll look like Mrs. 5x5. It is possible you might get away with this style in a coat where the length balances the width at the shoulders.

If you are big-hipped, don't have sleeves, jackets, belts, or other details that end at the hipline.

If you are big-bosomed, don't have sleeves that end at the bosom lines.

If you have a thin figure, you may add bulk with soft, blousy lines.

If you have a thick rib cage, a thickening waistline, or a protruding abdomen, hide them under an overblouse.

One could go on with similar advice ad infinitum. The message is

Fig. 11

clear; the eye will always do as directed. Lead it to your most interesting features; lead it away from those you would rather forget.

As the musician uses the notes of a scale, the writer words, so the designer uses *line* to express his ideas. Just as some painters delight us because they are great colorists, so some designers delight us because they are masters in the use of line. Balenciaga's clothes are pure line. So also are the works of the great American designers Norell, Galanos, and Tassell.

Shape and Space

A combination of lines produces shape. The most obvious and therefore the most important shape is the silhouette. Silhouettes change sometimes subtly, sometimes drastically. However they change, the history of costume design reveals that three main silhouettes recur in the fashion cycle—the straight or columnar (Fig. 12a), the bell or bouffant (Fig. 12b), and backswept fullness (Fig. 12c).

a   b   c

Fig. 12

Contemporary designs are based on all three (Fig. 13).

The vogue for geometric designs in both line and fabric favors, indeed requires, the simplicity of the columnar silhouette. While the "tent" silhouette appears new, it is in reality a kind of geometric simplification of the bell.

Fig. 13

PLAY WITHIN A PLAY

Style lines within the silhouette create other shapes (Fig. 14). The imaginative and playful quality of the shapes-within-shapes of current designs illustrates this delightfully. In many cases, if the lines of the design itself don't do it, the fabric does.

Fig. 14

The eye plays tricks with shapes as it does with lines. In the following illustration (Fig. 15) which of each pair looks bigger?

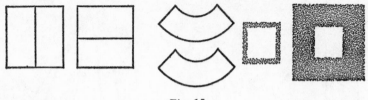

Fig. 15

Actually, each pair is the same size.

Which group of lines in Fig. 16 appears wider, which narrower?

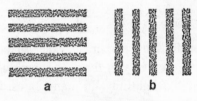

Fig. 16

Are you surprised that Fig. 16a appears narrower than Fig. 16b? You've always been taught that vertical lines make you look slimmer and horizontal lines make you look wider. In groups of lines it is not only the direction of the lines but the spaces between the lines which tell the eye how to move. When the eye moves easily without being stopped as in Fig. 16a, this group appears narrower. Where the eye movement is stopped, as by the end lines in Fig. 16b, the group appears wider.

A shape within a shape is contained in Figs. 17a and 17b. Which of these appears narrower?

Fig. 17

In Fig. 17a, the eye moves upward with the lines of the narrow central panel convincing us that the square is taller and narrower.

In Fig. 17b, the eye moves across the wide central panel, which fools us into thinking the square is wider.

Consider the effect of optical illusions in these dresses.

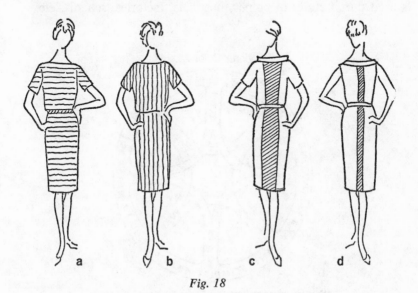

Fig. 18

Fig. 18a—The horizontal grouping of stripes actually makes this dress appear slimmer than Fig. 18b.

Fig. 18b—The vertical grouping of stripes makes this dress appear broader than Fig. 18a.

Fig. 18c—The wide central panel makes this dress seem wider than the one in Fig. 18d.

Fig. 18d—The narrow central panel makes this dress appear slimmer than the one in Fig. 18c.

Color as Illusion

When it comes to creating illusions, nothing beats color. Color can make people, objects, landscapes advance, recede, or disappear. Color can make the wearer bold or demure, tall or short, fat or thin. It's the greatest camouflage of all!

The eye reacts strongly to color. For instance: red, which has a strong impact on the visual center, is almost universally used as a signal for danger.

We react emotionally to colors (Fig. 19). Because of this, color is used purposefully in homes, hospitals, factories, schools, etc.

Emotional Color Wheel*

*Emotional Color Wheel, American Fabrics, Fall-Winter 1960, pg. 69

Fig. 19

The colors we wear not only affect the viewer, they also affect the wearer. One feels different when wearing a light, bright color than when wearing a dark or drab color.

We use colors as symbols. In our culture, white, which is "uncorrupted" light, is used as the color of purity. Hence, brides wear white. Black, which absorbs all color, is the "burial" of light. It is our color of mourning. We speak of "being in the pink" when we are feeling fine. We say we are "blue" when we are depressed.

Everyone knows that color has much to do with how well a person looks in her dress or suit or coat. But, did you also know that the fit of a garment may well be governed by its color? This makes it important to understand something of color theory.

THE TRIADIC COLOR THEORY

The hundreds of colors that delight us are derived from three basic colors—yellow, red, and blue. We call these *primary colors* because they cannot be obtained by mixing any colors (Fig. 20a). By combining any two of the primary colors, we create *secondary colors* (Fig. 20b). For instance, yellow and red produce orange. Yellow and blue make green. Red and blue yield violet.

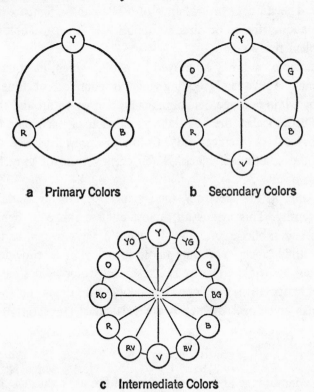

a   Primary Colors   b   Secondary Colors

c   Intermediate Colors

Fig. 20

Between the primary and secondary colors are the *intermediate* colors (Fig. 20c); yellow-green, blue-green, blue-violet, red-violet, red-orange, and yellow-orange. You could keep up this mixing of colors until you had every possible hue in the spectrum around the color wheel.

HUE, VALUE, AND INTENSITY

When we say red or violet or blue-green, we are referring to a *hue*. A hue may be light, spectrum, or dark—for instance: light blue, spectrum blue, dark blue. This lightness or darkness of a color is called *value*. Values may range from white to black but the color is still recognizable as the hue (except, of course, the white and the black).

Colors also have a quality of brightness or dullness. This is called *intensity*. The strength or brilliance of a hue can be tempered or subdued by adding the color directly opposite to it on the color wheel, its complementary color.

For example: red may be grayed by adding green, its complement. Yellow may be subdued by adding violet, its complement. Blue may be grayed by adding orange, its complement and so on around the color wheel. Theoretically, the just-right proportion of each pair of complementary colors produces gray. Colors are grayed as well as darkened by the addition of black. Black or any form of gray tends to neutralize a color.

Every hue in the spectrum, then, can appear in every value and every intensity. This means an almost endless range of light, dark, brilliant, and subtle colors. You may not always recognize them by their scientific labels. You may know them better as shocking pink, Alice blue, periwinkle, chartreuse, rust, etc. Color names can be descriptive, imaginative, or poetic. The people who dream up the names of lipsticks and fingernail polish are particularly inventive.

ADVANCING AND RECEDING COLORS

The golden orange of the sun, the red of fire are colors we associate with warmth. *The warm colors*—yellows, oranges, and reds—have a great luminosity. The eye sees them first. Artists call them *advancing colors*. The dark blue of night, the green-blue of water are colors we associate with coolness. *The cool colors*—the violets, the blues, the greens—are just the opposite of the warm colors. They retire to the background. Artists call them *receding colors*.

Scientists have long been intrigued by this phenomenon of advancing and receding colors. By actual scientific measurements they have discovered why they are so. They have found that the dominant hues —that is, the warm colors—have longer wavelengths, making them advance. The cool colors have shorter wavelengths, making them retire. So, if you want everyone to see you coming, wear a bright red dress (with a scientific blessing). But, if you would rather lose yourself in the crowd, wear a soft blue-violet.

Light values of a color will also make the color advance, while dark values make a color recede. People can spot you more easily in a pink tweed suit than in a deep garnet one.

Light colors reflect light; dark colors absorb it. We wear light colors in the summertime not only because they look cooler. They actually keep us cooler because they reflect the light (the warm rays of the sun). We wear dark colors in the wintertime not only because they look warmer. They actually are warmer because they absorb the light.

Because light colors reflect light they are flattering when worn close to the face. You've undoubtedly had this experience with a white collar or a white necklace. Because dark colors absorb light they rob the face of color. Black worn close to the face requires more makeup to compensate for the loss of color.

Light, bright, warm, advancing colors make the figure look heavier. Grayed, dark, cool, receding colors make it look slimmer. This is why you may look substantial in a white dress while everyone wants to know if you've lost weight when you wear your black one. With this in mind, you may want to fit your light, bright, warm-color dress closer to the figure to counteract the force of the color. You have more leeway with your dress of grayed, dark, cool, receding color.

We hasten to add that *normally* warm colors are advancing colors and cool colors are receding ones. This is not always so. We do not ever see colors in isolation. We see them in relationship to other colors. How a particular color appears to us is very much affected by its hue, value, intensity, and amount in relationship to the hue, value, intensity, and amount of surrounding colors. There is always an interaction between the two.

Picture a girl in a black bathing suit walking along a sandy beach. By all the rules, the sand, which is light and often fiercely reflects the light, should be the advancing color while the bathing suit, which is dark, should be the receding color. Just the opposite happens. The black color stands out (advances) against the sand color, which recedes. *A color advances or recedes in relation to the surrounding colors.*

COLOR COMBINATIONS THAT PRODUCE TONALITY

Many of us have been taught to think in terms of "color schemes." We are afraid to depart from combinations of colors that we are accustomed to seeing together. This is cliché color-thinking. A creative use of color provides the surprise of unexpected color combinations. The truth of the matter is that almost any colors can be used in combination if they are the correct value and intensity and are used in the right proportion.

Colors Used Side by Side in Combination Produce a Tonality. The eye rather than the artist does the mixing of colors. (This is the technique used by the Impressionist and pointillist painters.) For instance, a tweed fabric woven of red and blue yarns produces a color effect that is no longer either red or blue but a new color of violet tonality. Try matching thread or buttons to such a combination and you will soon discover this.

A Color Can Also Be Darkened by an Adjacent Color. A cloth woven of red and black yarns gives the appearance of dark red. *A color* can be *grayed by an adjacent color.* A fabric woven of gray and pink yarns looks like a warm gray.

A new color is produced when a transparent fabric of one color is used over another. A sky-blue dress has its skirt greened by a top layer of yellow chiffon.

COLOR COMBINATIONS THAT CONTRAST

For dramatic effect use colors that contrast or have shock value. The blue of the sky and the green of grass are nature's colors, yet their use together in clothing and in interiors is considered new and bold. Red and orange—side by side on the color wheel, related to each other by the common ingredient of red—still seem an exotic pairing. Both of these color combinations have a tendency to startle.

Contrast makes us see colors more sharply: the spotting of Somali leopard, a black and white rooster with his red beak and cockscomb, the view of earth from outer space—dark of night and light of day. Any two contrasting colors make each other more intense. A white coat worn over a black dress makes the white appear whiter and the black, blacker.

Complementary colors intensify each other. Christmas holly with its red berries and green leaves makes both the red and green brighter. Have you ever noticed how dressing rooms painted pink bring out the green in skin tones? If shops had any staff members who were knowledgeable about color, they would quickly repaint them a color more inclined to flatter.

A full intensity color seems even more brilliant when placed next to any neutralized tones. A blue blouse looks very blue when worn with a neutralized orange (brown).

A FEW THINGS TO REMEMBER IN CHOOSING CONTRASTING COLORS FOR COSTUMES

The eye is attracted to light, bright colors.

Light, bright areas seem larger than dark, dull areas of the same size.

A light central panel against a dark side section can make the figure appear slimmer.

Contrasting colors of bodice and skirt can make the figure appear shorter.

In the past few years, fashion has been a kaleidoscope. The use of color has been free, gay, bold, unafraid! The impact may have left some of us shattered at the very least, certainly not the same. In a world of color, it seems so unadventuresome to stick to the safe blacks, browns, and navys in an effort to appear trim or chic. Brighter colors can do as much—and perhaps more.

Texture

Perhaps you've had the experience of using the same pattern for two different fabrics. You know then how very different the resulting garments can be and how very different the problems of construction and fitting.

Texture is the structural quality of a fabric. It refers to whether the fabric is

shiny	or	dull
patterned	or	plain
open, airy, gauzy	or	heavy, dense, compact
translucent	or	opaque
supple, pliable, clinging	or	stiff, hard, firm
stretchable	or	unbudgeable
blistered, looped, fuzzed, raised, rough	or	flat, smooth

These textures give the illusion of size and bulk: lustrous fabrics which reflect the light, hard and stiff fabrics which conceal the figure, raised surfaces that increase the size of the wearer in proportion to the bulkiness of the cloth, fabrics with great surface interest in weave or design.

These textures appear to decrease the size of the figure: dull colors (as opposed to shiny; not to lack of interest), light or medium-weight fabrics, smooth surfaces, fabrics with less insistent surface interest in weave or design.

Transparent fabrics suggest and hint at the figure rather than completely revealing it. The size of the figure becomes indeterminate.

A Word About Patterned Areas—stripes, plaids, floral, or geometric motifs. Patterned areas must be used judiciously. Small designs tend to make an area appear smaller while large, bold motifs make it seem larger. One would think, then, that persons with large figures would do well to choose fabrics with small units in order to diminish their size and that those with small figures would choose the larger motifs in order to increase their size. Yet just the opposite happens: small innocuous designs are lost on the former and large motifs overpower the latter. The wiser choice is to select designs proportionate to the size of the figure.

Designs in closely related colors produce a color tonality rather than a patterned effect. For many figures, this is preferable to the shock of bold contrast.

If you are tall and slender, you can wear fabrics of any texture. If you tend to be heavy, select smooth, non-clinging fabrics without too much surface interest.

A short, stout person is better off choosing soft, pliable, less dense textures and retiring rather than aggressive patterned surfaces. (In fabric design, there really is such a thing as an aggressive flower.)

Fabrics with no "give" require more than normal ease.

Fabrics with stretchability require little ease.

Why do you suppose it is that the most alluring fabrics always seem to be those that add pounds to the figure?

Means to an End

These four elements—line, color, space, and texture—create their illusions by the skill with which they are used. This involves the further discussion of means: proportion, balance, unity and variety, emphasis and restraint.

PROPORTION

Your favorite recipe will tell you to use so many eggs to so much flour, or so large a roast for so many people. This is a matter of proportion. In design, proportion is the relationship of one part of a design to another. It may be the amount of bodice to length of skirt, the amount of light to dark, or the amount of one color to another.

In your costume, proportion is the size of your hat or bag in relationship to the rest of your costume. It may be the length of your jacket in relationship to the slimness or fullness of your skirt. It may be the amount of turquoise you are planning to wear with your black dress.

Proportion gives a new look to an old idea. That is why in fashion cycles, returning old ideas—long skirts, fitted bodices, exaggerated sleeves, etc.—have a new look. They come back but in not quite the same proportions.

The designer works for pleasing proportions in his design. The wearer must consider the rightness of the design to her own proportions. For she has them, too: her height to her width, her length from neckline to waist, from waist to toes, her width of shoulders, of bust, of waist, of hips, etc.

In design, an equal division of space or color tends to become monotonous (Fig. 21a). An unequal division of space is more interesting (Fig. 21b).

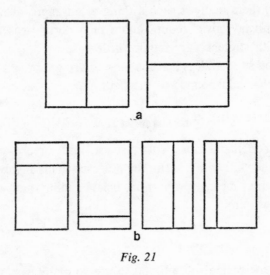

Fig. 21

Proportion involves balance; the two are inseparable. For example: a small area of strong color balances a large area of a less insistent color. Were the two to be used in equal proportions the effect of the strong color would be overpowering.

BALANCE

When we say that something is in balance we mean that no one part of it outweighs another in force or importance. We imply equality or equilibrium. This may or may not mean sameness on both sides of the scale.

Consider this: Jack and Jill are twins. They are as alike as two peas in a pod. They are the same height and the same weight. They like to do the same things. Here they are playing on a seesaw (Fig. 22a). The game is fun for them for they are evenly matched. This is a balance of equals.

Here is a drawing of an enlarged snowflake (Fig. 22b). The same

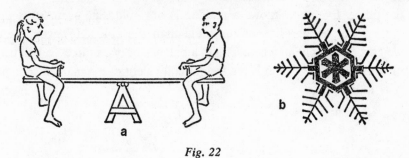

Fig. 22

design unit is repeated around its center. This is a balance of equal parts.

In both of these examples, balance is achieved by the exact duplication. In the case of Jack and Jill, the duplication is on either side of an axis. (An axis may be real or imaginary.) In the snowflake, an exact unit was repeated around a point. (The point may be imaginary as well as real.) Both of these display formal or symmetrical balance. This is the type of balance most generally used in clothing design (Fig. 23a).

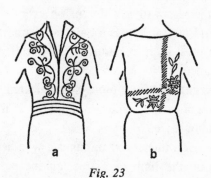

Fig. 23

In Fig. 23b, balance is achieved in another way. The right and left sides are different though equal. This is an informal or asymmetrical balance. It is a balance of equivalents.

Do you remember the story of the maiden who was worth her weight in gold? She sat on one side of the scale while the gold was heaped on the other. Everyone knows a maiden is not gold. She even takes up more room on her side of the scale than the gold. However, their weights are evenly matched. This is a balance of two unlikes, a balance of equivalents. The gold is the weight equivalent of the maiden though it is unlike her.

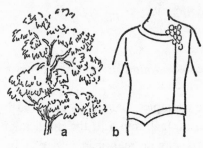

Fig. 24

There is a lovely dogwood tree in blossom in my garden. I look at it from my window. I walk around it on the terrace. From whatever spot I gaze, I see the masses of pink blossoms. Though always the same in beauty, their growth is different on every side. Yet the tree appears balanced (Fig. 24a). It is a balance of uneven parts, a "felt" balance, the type most seen in nature. This is called an informal or asymmetrical balance.

In clothing design, this is a more sophisticated type of balance (Fig. 24b) and requires great skill in handling. It is so easy to push it to a point of unbalance.

We are always made uneasy by unbalance whether it be too many little boys sitting on the limb of a tree, an inexperienced little girl stepping gayly into the prow of a canoe, or too much of anything in a costume.

The designer composes his space so that it is divided into interesting shapes and spaces in proportions that balance each other. He balances the lines and colors of his design. He chooses textures which balance. In a good design, all of the elements are in fine balance whether that balance be symmetrical or asymmetrical.

UNITY AND VARIETY

In addition to all of the other qualities mentioned, good design must also have unity and variety. Do they sound contradictory? Both are as necessary for art as they are for life. We are all enough alike to make communication and understanding possible. Yet, mentally, physically, and emotionally, we are all quite different. This makes life interesting. Unity and variety make design interesting, too.

Unity is a oneness, a belongingness whether it refers to international relations or only to this spring's costume. To achieve it there must be:

1. *A common or specific point of interest.*
   If you have decided that your new outfit is to be blue, then every part of your ensemble must contribute to the look of blue. This doesn't mean that everything must be blue; that would be monotonous. Any other color which is used must heighten or intensify the blue.

2. *Every detail of the ensemble must cooperate with every other one.*
   The type and size and color of your hat must not be at war with the color and texture and lines of your coat, while your bag and shoes are slugging it out on their own. They are all members of the same team and each must take its proper place and perform THE action required of it.

3. *Each part of the costume must be consistent with the rest.*
   You wouldn't think of wearing a pair of soiled sneakers with a pink peau de soie evening dress. This is an exaggerated example of inconsistency. You must be alert to the more subtle ones.

4. *There can be a unity of unlike but related parts.*
   Your new fall suit is a handsome tweed. With it you wear alligator shoes. Tweed and alligator are unlike in texture but they are related in character and function.

5. *There can be a unity of opposites.*
   An evening dress of black organza embroidered with rows of

glittering jet beads makes a memorable gown. The shininess of the beads and the dull matte surface of the organza are opposite in texture. Yet their use together produces harmony.

6. *There can be a unity of diversified elements.*
A flounced sundress has shoestring straps and a parade of buttons down the front, each of a different color. A diversity of elements, yes. But everything about the dress contributes to the theme of playfulness.

Relate—Don't Duplicate. Many women hope to achieve unity by making everything match—dress, coat, hat, bag, shoes. There is the ubiquitous pin-and-earrings set or matching necklace and earrings. This is an obvious kind of unity. It is true that unity comes with a repetition of color, line, shape, or texture. However, too much repetition can become monotonous.

A surprise touch, offbeat combinations of colors or textures, a print-and-plain can lend interest to an ensemble. This departure from sameness is variety. You remember the old saying, "Variety is the spice of life." So it is in your costume. Add a dash of color to spice it or a "smidgen" of texture to season it.

If too much sameness can make for dullness, too much variety can make for chaos. What is needed is a happy balance of the two.

AND HERE IS A FINAL PAIR TO CONSIDER—EMPHASIS AND RESTRAINT

Emphasis is dramatizing one element of design—color, line, texture. In a costume, emphasis could mean featuring *a* hat *or* dress *or* jewelry. If every part of the costume is shouting for attention it is impossible really to see any part of it. No matter how fine each individual detail may be, it loses something when it is thrust in competition with every other. "Too much of a muchness" is distracting.

Restraint is the other side of the coin. Emphasis of one element implies subordination of the rest. Restraint requires the removal of any element or detail which detracts from the center of interest or the main theme. There is always another time to make another statement. Understatement is a prominent ingredient of elegance.

How Does All of the Foregoing Theory Relate to Fitting?

One cannot really separate design and fit. Fit is part of the design; the design wouldn't look like *the* design without its intended fit. They must be judged as one.

Speaking in reference to the importance of a leg covering in relation to the short dress, Bill Blass, the great American designer, observed, "A designer can't even have a fitting on a dress today without the correct stockings" (New York *Times,* May 17, 1967).

Does this seem an extreme statement to you? It isn't really if one considers that top-to-toe continuity dictates not only the length of the skirt but the fit of dress, suit, or coat, which are, after all, only part of the total design.

To create the illusion of beauty, all of us work at tricking the eye into seeing what is or isn't there. We do this with line, with color, with space, with texture, with hope—and with art.

Chapter III

THE SHAPE OF FASHION

HOW TO MAKE A FLAT PATTERN FIT A NOT-SO-FLAT YOU

Mrs. Neanderthal's problems were simple. All she had to do was swing a fur skin over her curvaceous form, anchor it with a bone on one shoulder, and presto! there she was—seductively attired. No fuss about size or figure type. No to-do about seaming or shaping. Hers was a covering for all seasons, accommodating to all dimensions, large and small, and to all curves, big and little, concave and convex. The only real problem was whether to wear the fox for every day and the leopard on Sundays or vice versa.

Fig. 25

Pity us poor moderns! Fashions are such that even our semifitted and unfitted clothes must somehow be shaped to show off to best advantage one's height, width, depth, and the numerous curves contained within these dimensions.

Draping, the oldest and longest continuous means of shaping clothing, while seemingly simple in construction really depends on the skilled hands of the draper. Since he has only one pair of these gifted hands, his output is of necessity limited. Not so, the yards and yards of fabric and the hours and hours of time required for his creativity. These must be unlimited. This is hardly a method that lends itself to present-day production methods, either factory or home. Called for are some degree of uniformity, a minimum amount of fabric, a maximum amount of engineering, and the shortest possible construction time.

Dart Control

The blueprint by which this can be accomplished for manufacturer and home sewer alike is the flat block pattern based on the principle of *dart control*. By this scheme, a flat pattern (eventually a flat length of cloth) can be shaped to fit a not-so-flat figure.

Dart Control Always Represents a Relationship. It is the difference between a larger measurement and a smaller adjoining one. For instance, if the bust measures 35 inches and the waistline 27 inches, the dart control necessary to shape the bodice is 8 inches. If the waist measures 27 inches and the hips 37 inches, the dart control necessary to shape the skirt is 10 inches. The greater the difference, the larger the amount of control; the smaller the difference, the smaller the amount of control.

There is this too: the larger the amount of stitched dart control, the greater the bulge which is produced. The smaller the amount of stitched dart control, the less the bulge created.

The important thing to remember is that it is not whether a figure is short or tall, heavy or slim which determines the amount of shaping or dart control. It is always *the relationship between two adjoining measurements*. For instance,

a petite figure with a 22-inch waist and 27-inch hips needs 5 inches
for dart control. So does a heavy figure with a 38-inch waist and
43-inch hips.

Fig. 26

A differential in measurements is found wherever in the body there
are curves or high points or bulges. The most obvious curve is the
circumference of the body. Within this somewhat cylindrical form
there are a series of secondary curves. There are eight such places in

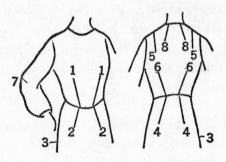

Fig. 27

1. bust,   2. abdomen,   3. side hip,   4. buttocks,   5. upper shoulder blades,
6. lower shoulder blades,   7. elbow,   8. dowager's hump (back of neck).

a woman's body that concern the patternmaker and that call for dart control (Fig. 27).

When you come to think of it aren't these the places where you have always found some shaping in your clothing (Fig. 28)?

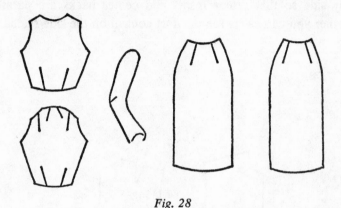

Fig. 28

In a pattern you will find darts and seams (or some equivalent, see page 50) in corresponding places (Fig. 29).

Fig. 29

The total amount of dart control is divided three ways—front, back, and side. In the bodice, since the bust needs the most shaping, the largest amount of control is placed in front. In the skirt, since the buttocks require the most shaping, the largest amount of control is placed in back. If you place the front and back bodices and skirts side by side so that center fronts and center backs are parallel to each other you can easily see the dart control on the side seams (Fig. 30).

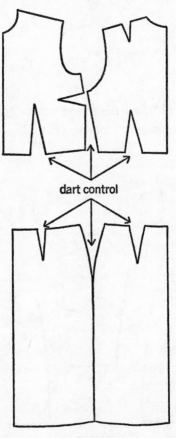

Fig. 30

Dart Control Is the Key to Good Fitting. The amount and placement of it is a very personal matter. You *must* do the following:

1. Find the right amount of dart control for your figure and allocate it correctly—front, back, and side.

2. Position the dart control where it is needed—the high points of your curves.

(A well-fitted basic pattern is an excellent permanent record of this. It can be used as a guide for adjusting style patterns. Directions for making a basic pattern will be found in Chapter VI.)

If a pattern or garment has too much dart control for your figure, it will create bulges where there are none. If you have a curvy figure and use a pattern (or choose a garment) that does not have enough dart control for you, there will not be sufficient shaping. When dart control is improperly placed, it releases fullness where you may not need it and deprives you of it where you do need it (Fig. 31).

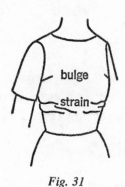

Fig. 31

Now examine some of the clothes you have made or bought. Are the darts and shaping seams in the right places (see page 135) and in the right amounts for you?

The most obvious, usual, and simplest form in which dart control appears is in darts (Fig. 32a). This makes for rather elementary design. Most designers prefer to incorporate the control in shaping seams (Fig. 32b). Not all seams in a design are shaping seams. Some are merely style lines. You must learn to distinguish between them (see page 62).

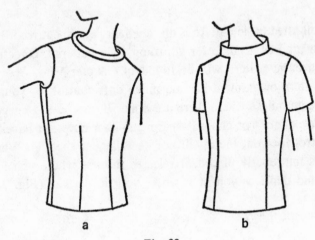

Fig. 32

Darts and seams are not the only ways to control shaping. Dart tucks (Fig. 33a), pleats—either pressed or unpressed (Fig. 33b), shirring (Fig. 33c), and smocking (Fig. 33d) are alternate ways.

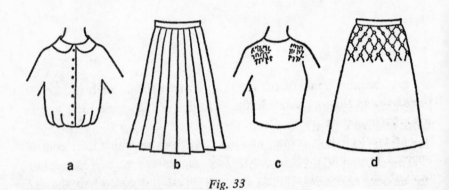

Fig. 33

DESIGN BY DARTS

Designers think of many complex, ingenious, and unobvious ways to shape the garment. It becomes a challenge to them to conceal the structure in a decorative manner. Any device will do as long as it "takes in" the amount needed to make the garment fit the smaller measurement and "lets it out" at the right place to fit the larger measurement.

The fascinating thing about dart control is that while the amount of it is a constant (established for your figure), it may appear in a variety of places. Darts may be placed in any position as long as they follow this rule: they must start from some seam and extend to the high point of the curve under consideration. This means that a dart can emerge from any point on the circumference of bodice front, bodice back, skirt front, skirt back, and sleeve. For example: you've undoubtedly seen designs which utilize the bodice front dart control in any one of the positions indicated in Fig. 34a.

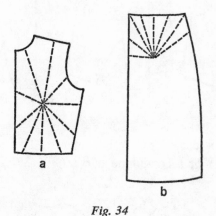

Fig. 34

Exactly the same thing can be done with the bodice back, the skirt front and back (Fig. 34b), and the sleeve. This positioning also holds for pleats, dart tucks, shirring, smocking, etc.

The shifting of the dart control to new positions in no way alters the amount of control. It does alter the shape of the pattern piece and, of course, the design. To have a dart in a new position makes a new design (Fig. 35).

Fig. 35

In most patterns the dart legs are straight lines (Fig. 36a). There is some ease when a dart has straight legs. When more shaping and less ease is desired, the dart legs may be curved to the shape of the body (Fig. 36b).

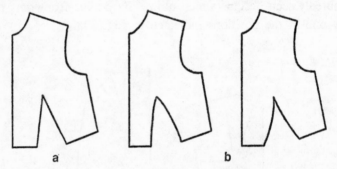

Fig. 36

Often a dart is curved for design interest. This may be a simple curve (Fig. 37a) or a compound curve (Fig. 37b).

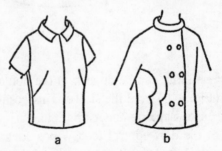

Fig. 37

SHAPING SHOULD SUIT THE FABRIC

Any dart (or shaping seam) will interrupt the continuity of the fabric design. Therefore you must choose a pattern with darts or seams which will do so with the least disturbing effect. When you are using a solid-color fabric, there is no problem. When you are using a figured material—a spaced print of either large or small units; a stripe, a check, a plaid; a visible vertical, horizontal, or diagonal weave—then the choice of dart or control seams becomes more complex.

Often, simply shifting the existing dart to a new position will produce a more pleasing effect. For example:

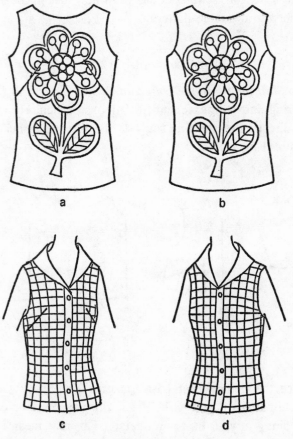

a   b

c   d

Fig. 38

The darts in Fig. 38a cut into the floral motif. Would you deliberately cut a flower apart if it were real? Why do it in the fabric? Shifting the darts to a new position (Fig. 38b) leaves the motif intact while preserving the original dart control. This is certainly a satisfactory arrangement for the floral fabric as well as you.

The position of the darts in Fig. 38c results in a mismatching of the fabric design. Balancing the horizontal and/or vertical darts on the straight lines of the fabric produces a more pleasing effect while preserving the dart control.

There are many times when it is advisable to shift the dart control to a position more consistent with the fabric design. Often, too, one finds that a particular dart or a combination of darts is more flattering. For these reasons sewers should know how to shift the dart control in an otherwise desirable pattern.

HOW TO SHIFT THE DART CONTROL

How to Shift the Waistline Dart to a French Underarm Dart. (This is a flattering dart with excellent fit. It looks particularly well in profile. The direction of the line suggests the lift one associates with a high, youthful figure.)

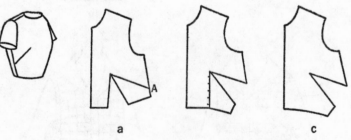

a   c

Fig. 39

1. Trace the bodice-front basic pattern. You may work directly with a style pattern if you wish. If you do, you must be certain that the dart point is at your bust point height. This may mean lengthening or shortening the dart before you can make any changes.

2. Cut out the tracing and the dart. In the style pattern, cut out the dart.

3. Locate the point from which the new dart will enter the bodice. Mark this point A.

4. Draw a line connecting the dart point with A (Fig. 39a).

5. Slash on this line. Slash up to the dart point but not through it.

6. Using the dart point as a pivot, close the original dart. Scotch tape it to position (Fig. 39b). The new dart will appear in the desired position. It will automatically contain the proper amount of dart control.

This shifting of dart control is a great revelation to most home sewers. Also fun. If you run true to form you will be eager to try out this new-found information immediately. Why not try shifting darts to other positions by this same procedure?

HOW TO DIVIDE THE DART CONTROL

Sometimes the amount of dart control is just too much for a single dart. It produces too great a bulge when more gradual shaping is preferable. Or, it throws off the grain at a seam line with resulting bias pull. To avoid either of these contingencies the dart control may be divided.

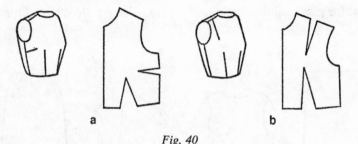

a   b

Fig. 40

On the bodice front, the dart control is frequently divided between waistline and underarm darts (Fig. 40a) or waistline and shoulder darts (Fig. 40b).

This Is How the Division Is Made

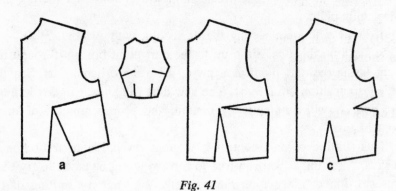

Fig. 41

Steps 1 to 5 are the same as for shifting the dart control (see page 54).

6. Close *part* of the original dart control, shifting the remainder to the new position (Fig. 41b).

Fig. 41c shows the pattern with shortened darts.

MULTIPLE DARTS

The dart control may also be divided into several darts on the same seam line (Fig. 42). This is done for several reasons: for design interest, for more subtle shaping, for more pleasing use of the patterned surface of a fabric.

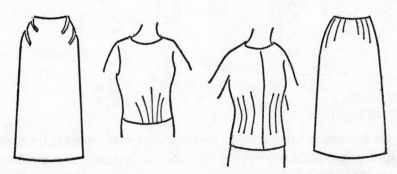

Fig. 42

Here is *an easy way* for non-patternmakers *to make multiple darts.* This method can *only* be used *for darts on the same seam line.*

1. Trace the dart on another piece of paper. Cut it out (Fig. 43a).

2. Divide the cut-out dart into the desired number of parts (Fig. 43b). Cut them apart. In each new dart you will find that one dart leg is shorter than the other.

3. Make the dart legs equal in length (Fig. 43c).

4. Set the new darts into position on the pattern on either side of the bust point (X) and about 1 inch apart at the seam (Fig. 43d).

5. Trace the new darts in their new positions (Fig. 43d).

Should there be three darts, place one at the bust point and one on either side of it.

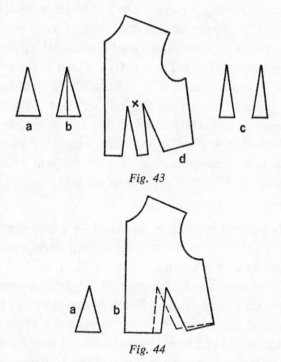

Fig. 43

Fig. 44

TO RELOCATE A DART

The paper dart device is an easy way to relocate a dart when the existing dart would serve better if repositioned on the same seam line.

1. Trace the dart on another piece of paper. Cut it out (Fig. 44a).

2. Place the cut-out dart on the pattern in the desired new position and trace (Fig. 44b). The broken line in the illustration is the original dart; the solid line is the newly placed dart.

DESIGNER'S DARTS VS. DRESSMAKER'S DARTS

All pattern changes—shifting, slashing, dividing—are made from the high points of the darts. In dressmaking or tailoring, however, darts are seldom worn stitched to these heights. That would be asking too much of most figures. The darts are shortened for a softer effect and a little more ease.

The darts that extend to the high points are called *designer's darts*. They are used in *making a pattern*. Only in small or youthful figures and only in very fitted garments are darts stitched to these high points.

The more general shortened darts used in dressmaking and tailoring are called *dressmaker's darts*. *These* darts are used in the *making of a garment*. All darts on commercial patterns are shortened darts.

Here is a guide for shortening the designer's darts to convert them into dressmaker's darts. Do remember that "standard" lengths may be meaningless when applied to individual requirements. Take into consideration your figure, the type of garment, and your personal preference in fit. Shorten your darts in an amount that looks best and that feels most comfortable.

Bodice. Front-waistline dart is shortened $\frac{1}{2}$ inch from bust-point height. Back-waistline dart is shortened 1 inch from shoulder-blade height. Underarm dart is shortened 2 or more inches from the bust point. (This dart always ends at bust-point height no matter what the point of origin on the side seam.) Heavy-bosomed figures may bring this dart closer to the bust point if the garment fits better so.

French underarm dart (an exception) may be stitched to the bust point except in larger figures when it is shortened $\frac{1}{2}$ inch or more.

Front shoulder dart is shortened 2 inches or more from the bust point. Back shoulder dart is usually stitched to a finished length of 3 inches.

Sleeve. Elbow dart is usually stitched to $2\frac{1}{2}$-inch finished length.

Skirt. Front-skirt dart is shortened 2 inches from the high point of the front hipbone.

Back-skirt dart is shortened 1 inch from the high point of the buttock. Frequently skirt darts fit better when unshortened so that the dart releases the greatest amount of material where the figure is fullest. Use your judgment as to the best length for you.

How to Shorten a Dart

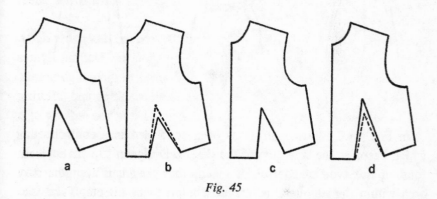

a   b   c   d

Fig. 45

1. Measure down from the dart point the amount you wish to shorten the dart. Mark the new dart point in the center of the space (Fig. 45a).
2. Draw new dart legs (Fig. 45b).

Should you need to do just the opposite, this is the way *to lengthen a dart.*

1. Measure directly up from the dart point the amount you wish to lengthen the dart. Mark the new dart point (Fig. 45c).
2. Draw new dart legs starting at the ends of the original dart (Fig. 45d).

The broken lines in Figs. 45b and d represent the original darts. The solid lines, the new darts.

Look, Ma, No Darts

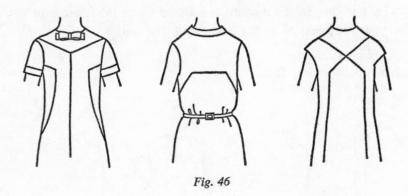

Fig. 46

In Fig. 46 the dart control has been concealed in a control seam which becomes the style line of the design. Designers are particularly fond of this type of control. It means that they can approach the area within the silhouette as an artist approaches his empty canvas. Unencumbered by those short dart-jabs, the designer is free to create interesting shapes and divisions with lines that intrigue him. Incorporating the control into these style lines becomes much more of a challenge. The resulting design is vastly more interesting to both its creator and wearer.

Control seams not only produce a beautiful flow of line but they are excellent opportunities for fitting. Some figures are so shaped that if there is no control seam, one would be well advised to create one. For example: A narrow-shouldered, heavy-bosomed figure not only looks better (Fig. 47a) in a design with control seams but the garment actually fits better than one with darts (Fig. 47b). A large-bosomed, slim-hipped figure not only looks better when a waistline dart in a sheath is extended as a control seam (Fig. 47c) but it is actually the only way the sheath will fit well. Without the control seam, the waistline dart creates a needless and unsightly bulge in the skirt (Fig. 47d).

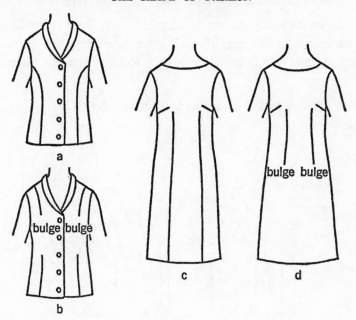

Fig. 47

The control seam is produced by dividing the dart control (Fig. 48a). Instead of stitching the two resulting darts, the pattern is separated (Fig. 48b). Seam allowance is added (Fig. 48c). The pattern sections are joined by this seam. Now, it is the control seam that does the shaping of the garment instead of darts.

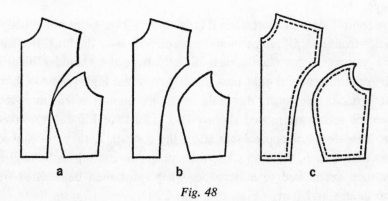

Fig. 48

Not all seams in a garment are control seams. Some are style lines. It is important to distinguish which seam lines carry the burden of the shaping and which are there merely to carry out the design.

How to Tell a Shaping Seam from a Style Line

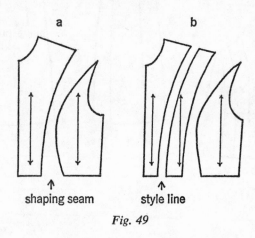

Fig. 49

Place the adjoining pattern sections side by side with the grain lines parallel to each other. You can see immediately if there is dart-like shaping in the seam (Fig. 49a). If there is, the seam can be used for fitting. When the lines are exactly alike, there is no control in the seam (Fig. 49b); it cannot be used for fitting without altering the design.

A control seam fits best when it falls across a high point of the body. Bodice-front control seams should pass directly over the bust. Bodice-back control seams should pass directly over the shoulder blades. Skirt control seams should pass directly over the high points of hips and buttocks. However, the design of a garment is often improved when the seams are moved slightly (no more than 1 inch) to either side. This does not appreciably affect the control. If they are moved more than 1 inch, the seams lose their power to control to the degree that they are moved to either side. They must then be assisted by other seams and darts (Figs. 50a and 50b).

a   b

Fig. 50

From the standpoint of fit, a control seam or a combination of darts is better than a single dart. A single dart if large enough may produce a sharp bulge. Several darts or control seams produce more subtle shaping. The more darts or control seams, the more opportunities for fitting. (There are limits. Too many darts and style lines in one garment produce a "busy" effect.)

In style periods when fitted clothing is the vogue, more shaping, therefore more dart control is necessary. In periods characterized by a more relaxed look, less dart control is used.

In selecting a pattern, study it carefully for the ways in which it will shape the garment. If your figure definitely requires shaping, don't succumb to a design that has no darts or seams unless you intend to create them on your own. On the other hand, if you have a flat, little figure, don't select something with a multitude of darts and shaping seams. Wherever and in whatever form it appears, the dart control is always there to do the shaping—simply in some designs, intricately in others.

Some sewers approach darts as if they were put there by an act of Congress and must never be moved or tampered with without official sanction. You need not be a slave to a pattern. Change it to fit you. Darts and control seams are there to do the shaping *for you*. They are waiting to be used *by you*. All it takes to change a pattern for the better is a little arithmetic, a little courage, a little judgment—and the information that follows in Chapter IV.

Chapter IV

A BLUEPRINT FOR FASHION
FITTING

HOW TO ALTER THE PATTERN TO FIT THE FIGURE

You're sunk if any major changes have to be made after the garment
has been cut. The best one can hope for then is to make minor changes
in the seam allowances and perhaps even sneak a little of the darts.
The size, the ease, the shaping, the placement of the silhouette seams,
the leeway for more flattering fit—all the criteria by which good fit can
be judged—have already been fixed by the cut-out pattern. This being
so it makes sense to get the pattern adjusted as close to the figure as
measurements and mathematics can make it.

You may know from previous experience what changes need to be
made in your patterns. However, a checkup should prove helpful.
The following list of measurements, lengthy though it is, by no means
exhausts the list of possible body measurements necessary to produce
a true duplication of your figure. It is comprehensive enough, however, to enable you to alter standard-size patterns so that they come
close to your own measurements. It also provides the information
you need for making a basic pattern.

. . . And a Yard Wide!

HOW TO TAKE YOUR BODY MEASUREMENTS

You will need help with this, since there are some measurements
you cannot possibly take for yourself. It is a good plan to get several

sewers together who will take measurements and who will learn to fit each other. ("Sewing Buddies" are a godsend!) It really is more fun this way, too. It takes some of the sting out of this painful procedure to discover that all the rest of the girls are in the same sorry predicament. Swear each other to eternal secrecy and begin!

Don't expect too much of yourself or your friends. You would need to be a professional measurement-taker with a thorough training and considerable experience behind you to achieve 100 percent accuracy.

In preparing your personal measurement chart, you will find two lists of measurements. The first list is a simpler one. There are fewer and less complex measurements to take. To compensate there is a heavy reliance on the fabric fitting. If you are better with fabric in-the-hand than with arithmetic, choose this list. If you are the precision type take the optional measurements, too. This should produce a garment very close to your figure even before the fitting.

WHO—ME?

One of the most difficult things in the world to face is a measurement. What that red matador's cape is to the bull, so that little number on the tape measure is to a woman—positively infuriating.

This is the moment of truth. But, if you want clothes that fit you—the present you, not the one you could be if you lost ten pounds—you must face the facts.

MAKE A CHART FOR YOURSELF LIKE THE FOLLOWING

The best measurements are taken in the foundation garments you generally wear (if you wear them)—bra, girdle, slip. Wear shoes of the heel height you favor; posture affects some of the measurements.

Personal Measurements Charts

GENERAL CIRCUMFERENCE MEASUREMENTS

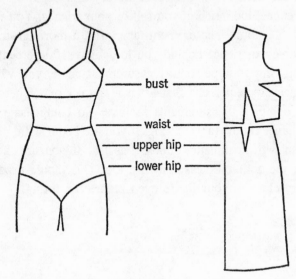

bust

waist
upper hip
lower hip

Fig. 51
Body measurements and corresponding position on pattern

Item	Me	Ease for Dress	Ease for Jacket	Ease for Coat	Total Needed	Pattern Measures	+ or −
1. BUST—taken over the crest of the bust and across the shoulder blades		3″	4″	4–5″			
2. WAIST—taken snugly while standing—in the hollow of the waist or where you would like the waistline to be in the garment		0–½″	1–1½″	2–2½″			
		a waist measurement taken while seated automatically adds the necessary amount of ease					
3. UPPER HIPS*—taken over the high point of the hipbone; note how much below the waistline							

Item	Me	Ease for Dress	Ease for Jacket	Ease for Coat	Total Needed	Pattern Measures	+ or −
4. LOWER HIPS*—taken around the fullest part of the hips; note how much below the waistline		2"	3"	3–4"			

Now: Tie a piece of string or pin a length of tape around your waist and another around the base of the neck. Push the waistline string or tape into the position you want for the waistline. The neckline tape should go from the socket (prominent) bone in back to the hollow between the collar bones in front. These provide fixed points from which and to which you may measure.

THE BODICE

Measurements Necessary for Simple Pattern Changes (Fig. 52)

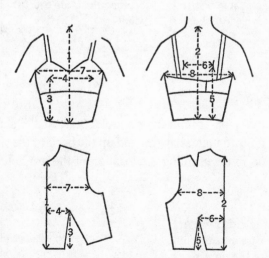

Body measurements and corresponding position on pattern

Fig. 52

* These two hip measurements help to determine the curve of the hip on the side seam.

Item	*Me*	*Ease*	*Total Needed*	*Pattern Measures*	*+ or −*
1. CENTER FRONT—from the base of the neck (the hollow between the collar bones) to the waist		0–½″			
2. CENTER BACK—from the socket bone to the waist		0–½″			
3. BUST-POINT HEIGHT—from the highest point of the bust straight to the waist; do not follow the contour of the bust		proportionate to over-all length			
4. BUST-POINT WIDTH—from bust point to bust point		proportionate to over-all width			
5. SHOULDER-BLADE HEIGHT —from the prominent or fleshy part of the shoulder blade to the waist		proportionate to over-all length			
6. SHOULDER-BLADE WIDTH —from shoulder blade to shoulder blade		proportionate to over-all width			

ARMHOLE TAPE

Pin a length of tape around the armhole. Start at the shoulder socket bone, bring it down under the arm and up the back to the shoulder bone. This is helpful in determining the location of the armhole seam.

7. ACROSS-THE-CHEST WIDTH —from the crease where arm meets body to the opposite crease (at the armhole tape); this is a surface measurement —do not extend it to the under-arm					

Item	*Me*	*Ease*	*Total Needed*	*Pattern Measures*	*+ or −*
8. ACROSS-THE-SHOULDER-BLADES WIDTH—with arms moderately forward, measure from the crease where arm meets body to the opposite crease (at the armhole tape)— also a surface measurement		ease is automatically added by the forward position of the arms; problem figures may add ½–1″ more			

Optional Measurements for More Complex Pattern Changes. For complete accuracy, fixed points are necessary from which and to which measurements can be taken. The shoulder socket, the back neck socket, the collar bones, the bust points, the shoulder blades, the hip-bones or abdomen, the buttocks, must all be marked. So also should

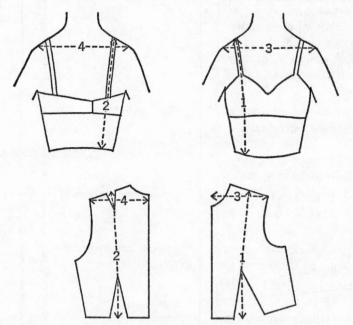

Body measurements and corresponding position on pattern
Fig. 53

be the shoulder seam, the armhole, the neckline, the bustline, the waistline, the hipline.

Lipstick, eye liner, or stick eye shadow are great for markings which fall on skin. They are safe and easily removed. Small safety pins are excellent for pinpointing (naturally) those points which are concealed by clothing. Heavy string or tape are good for locating the neckline, bustline, armhole, waistline, and hipline. A slip that fits well (a dress or skirt will do also) can be used for determining the side seams.

In order to take the following measurements (Fig. 53), you must first locate the shoulder seam. The *shoulder seam* extends from the shoulder socket to the base of the neck (established by the tape) *slightly* forward of the trapezius muscle.

Item	Me	Ease	Total Needed	Pattern Measures	+ or −
1. OVER-BUST LENGTH—from the middle of the shoulder seam over the highest point of the bust, straight to the waist; do not follow the contour of the bust		½″			
2. OVER-THE-SHOULDER-BLADE LENGTH—from the middle of the shoulder seam over the highest point of the shoulder blades to the waist		½″			
3. UPPER-FRONT width—from one shoulder point (socket) to the other		proportionate to over-all width ease			
4. UPPER-BACK width—from one shoulder point (socket) to the other; this is a slightly curved line		proportionate to over-all width ease			
5. SHOULDER POINT TO BUST POINT—this measurement helps to determine the slope of the shoulder line		no ease			

THE SKIRT (Fig. 54)

Measurements for Simple Pattern Changes

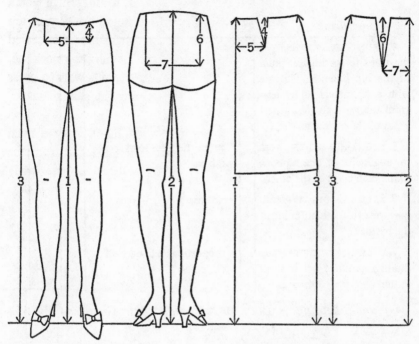

Body measurements   Corresponding position on pattern

Fig. 54

Item	Me	Ease	Total Needed	Pattern Measures	+ or −
1. CENTER-FRONT LENGTH—from the waist to the floor subtract the number of inches skirt is worn from the floor		no ease for length measurements			
2. CENTER-BACK LENGTH—from the waist to the floor; subtract the number of inches from the floor skirt is worn					
3. SIDE LENGTH—from the waist to the floor; subtract the number of inches from the floor the skirt is worn					

Item	Me	Ease	Total Needed	Pattern Measures	+ or −
4. FRONT-HIP DEPTH—from the waist to the highest point of the hip bone; in a figure with a prominent abdomen—from the waist to the highest point of the abdomen.					
5. FRONT-HIP WIDTH—from the highpoint of one hipbone to the high point of the other		proportionate—to over-all width ease			
6. BACK-HIP DEPTH—from the waist to the high point of the buttock		no ease			
7. BACK-HIP WIDTH—from the high point of one buttock to the other		proportionate to over-all width ease			

Optional Measurements for More Complex Skirt Changes (Fig. 55)

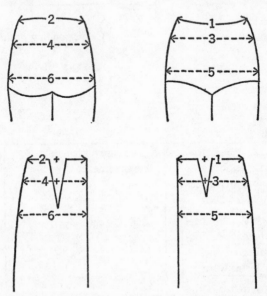

Body measurements and corresponding position on pattern
Fig. 55

Item	Me	Ease	Total Needed	Pattern Measures	+ or −
1. FRONT-WAIST WIDTH— from side seam to side seam at the waistline		0–¼″			
2. BACK-WAIST WIDTH—from side seam to side seam at the waistline		0–¼″			
3. FRONT-UPPER-HIP WIDTH —from side seam to side seam at upper-hip level		proportionate ease as side seam tapers from lower hipline to waistline			
4. BACK-UPPER-HIP WIDTH— from side seam to side seam at upper-hip level					
5. FRONT-LOWER-HIP WIDTH —from side seam to side seam at lower hip level		1″			
6. BACK-LOWER-HIP WIDTH —from side seam to side seam at lower-hip level		1″			

Despite what you may imagine, the correct placement of the side seams makes the skirt front generally one inch wider than the skirt back.

SLEEVE MEASUREMENTS (Fig. 56)

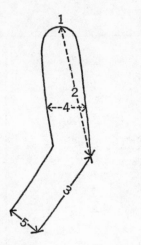
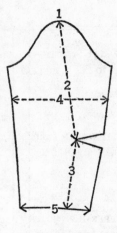

Body measurements   Corresponding position on pattern

Fig. 56

Item	Me	Ease for Dress	Ease for Jacket	Ease for Coat	Total Needed	Pattern Measures	+ or −
1. OVER-ARM LENGTH—with the arm bent—from the shoulder socket, to the elbow, to the wrist at the little finger		the bent arm provides the ease					
2. SHOULDER TO ELBOW—while the tape measure is still in position note this measurement							
3. ELBOW TO WRIST—the difference between the over-arm measurement and the shoulder-to-elbow measurement							

Item	Me	Ease for Dress	Ease for Jacket	Ease for Coat	Total Needed	Pattern Measures	+ or −
4. BICEPS—around the heaviest part of the upper arm; usually about midway between elbow and shoulder		2″	2½″	3″			
5. KNUCKLE CIRCUMFERENCE—around the fullest part of the hand as you would slip the hand through a sleeve		½″					

PANTS, AND VARIATIONS THEREOF

From the scrambling-after-the-kids, common garden variety blue jeans to the glamorous palazzo pajamas, pants have become the uniform of a whole generation of young women. Out of the realm of strictly sports, casual, or at-home wear, chic tailored pants suits have even moved into town. The enthusiasm for pants—short, long, or in between—is very understandable. For many activities, they are THE answer to the question of comfort. The "Should women wear pants?" debate has been relegated to the history books along with red flannels, long underwear, and high button shoes. The only real problems are how to choose from the many handsome versions now available and how to make them fit in the most flattering manner.

The Seat of the Trouble. Pants present the same fitting problems as skirts plus a few more. Those "few more" require some additional measurements (Fig. 57).

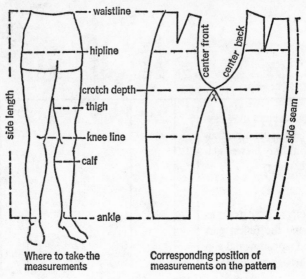

Where to take the measurements

Corresponding position of measurements on the pattern

Fig. 57

Measurement Chart for Pants and Variations Thereof

Item	Me	Ease	Total Needed	Pattern Measures	+ or −
1. WAIST—see chart page 72.					
2. UPPER HIPS—see page 72.					
3. LOWER HIPS—see page 72.					
4. THIGH—fullest part of upper leg		1″			
5. KNEE—taken with knee bent		any amount			
6. CALF—at heaviest part—usually mid-calf		either			
7. ANKLE—circumference at anklebone		comfortable or fashionable			
8. SIDE LENGTH—waist to desired length at side seam					

Item	Me	Ease	Total Needed	Pattern Measures	+ or −
9. KNEE LINE—from waist to knee on side seam					
10. CROTCH DEPTH—See Fig. 58 and accompanying directions		½–1"			
11. INSIDE-SEAM LENGTH—measure along inside leg from crotch to desired length					

CROTCH MEASUREMENT (Fig. 58)

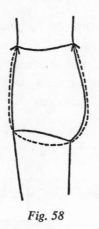

Fig. 58

Total Crotch Measurement—while standing, measure the distance from front waistline to back waistline between the legs (Fig. 58). Add 1½ to 2 inches for ease.

Crotch Length—Front—the front portion of the preceding measurement to the center of the inner thigh.

Crotch Length—Back—the difference between the total crotch length and the front crotch length.

It would be well to take the previous measurements over the foundation garments (if any) to be worn with the pants.

NOTE: Slacks and shorts are drafted so that the center back curve is longer and deeper than the center front curve. This longer, deeper center back seam provides the length required to accommodate the buttocks when seated. This also makes the back of slacks wider than the front, unlike the skirt where the front is larger than the back.

Had you ever realized there were so many points on the body and on the pattern that could and should be measured? It is the correct relationship between the body measurements and the pattern measurements that is the first giant step in making the garment fit you.

Compare Your Pattern with Your Measurements

In making the comparison between your body measurements and the pattern remember that:

The *pattern* generally represents only *half the width measurements*. Your *body measurements are whole measurements*. You will need to halve your width measurements to correspond to those of the pattern.

The *pattern* has *shortened darts*. *Your measurements* are for actual *high points*. Here's how to locate your dart points on the pattern (Fig. 59).

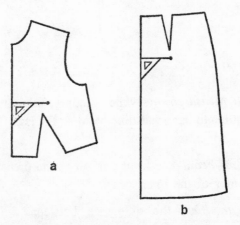

a

b

Fig. 59

BODICE (Fig. 59a)

On the center front or back, measure up from the natural waistline a distance equal to the bust or shoulder-blade height Square a line from this point over (see page 102) equal to half the bust or shoulder-blade width.

SKIRT (Fig. 59b)

On the center front or back, measure down from the natural waistline a distance equal to the front hip or buttocks depth. Square a line from this point over equal to half the front hip or buttocks width.

The *pattern* contains *all the necessary ease. You* must *add* the necessary *ease* to your measurements.

The waist is usually indicated on the pattern. The hip measurement is across the fullest part of a fitted skirt pattern.

In a pattern with control seams, the dart point height and width are at the fullest part of the curve of the seamline.

When a garment has a dropped neckline, it is difficult to determine the center-front and center-back lengths. The drop may be anything the designer wanted it to be whereas pattern measurements refer to a line around the base of the neck. One must be guided by past experience. If you generally lengthen or shorten your bodice, do so now.

1. Assemble all the parts which complete each unit of your garment, that is—bodice front, bodice back, skirt front, skirt back, and sleeve. Or, in the case of pants, all the sections that complete the front and back.

2. *Measure only that part of the pattern which will appear on the surface of the finished garment. Do not measure anything which will end up in some seam or dart or that will overlap another part.* Use your tape measure like an adding machine starting each new measurement at the end point of the previous one.

FOR EXAMPLE:

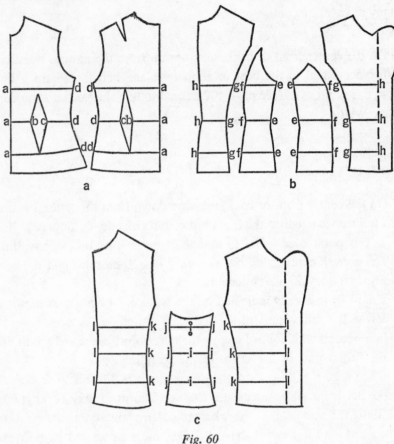

Fig. 60

Fig. 60a. Measure from the center front to the dart (a to b), from the dart to the side seam (c to d), or from the center front and back to the side seam (a to d).

Fig. 60b. Measure from seam line to seam line (e to f), from seam line to center front or back (g to h). Measurements go only to the line on which the garment will close. An extension either front or back laps over a part of the garment already measured.

Fig. 60c. Measure from underarm marking to seam line (i to j), from seam line to center front or back (k to l).

3. *Decide where and how much the pattern needs adjustment.* Too many changes or consistent over-all changes of 2 inches or more indicate you would be better off with the next size pattern. This does not apply where most of the pattern fits but some 2 inch changes must be made.

Learn to distinguish which elements of the pattern have style meaning and which are meant essentially for fit. In some styles the structure (which can be changed for fitting purposes) is hidden in control seams which in turn appear as style lines. In some designs, the style lines have nothing to do with the structure. They are superimposed as decorative lines only. These cannot be used for fitting. When a style line passes over or very close to a high point of the body chances are that it is a line that can be used for fitting. (See page 62 "How to Tell a Shaping Seam from a Style Line.") At this time, it is better to change the pattern only for fit. Style changes can be better determined after a trial muslin fitting.

Pattern changes are very specific. Make them only *if* and *where* you need them. Don't alter the entire pattern merely to get at one small change; this will throw out the fit entirely.

When there is more than one change, make each separately, one at a time. Don't try to do everything at once. It is generally easier to make lengthwise adjustments first, then the width adjustments.

When you make a change in a pattern piece, remember to make a corresponding change in the piece that joins it. For instance: a change in a neckline means a change in the neckline facing and/or the collar; a change in the sleeve cap means a change in the armhole. And so on.

General Procedure for Pattern Changes

Since it is humanly impossible to anticipate all the myriad needs of all individuals who require pattern changes, the best one can hope to do is to provide the basic principles, to describe the general procedures, and to show how they apply to some of the most frequently met figure problems.

CHANGES MAY BE MADE ON ANY OUTSIDE LINE OF A PATTERN (Fig. 61).

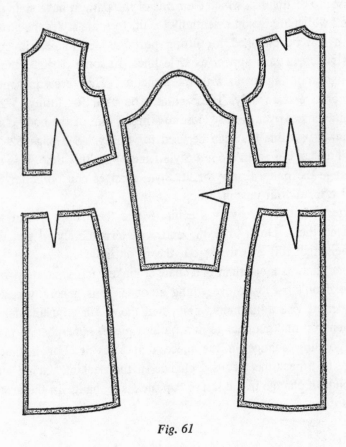

Fig. 61

If the design has control seams, you have that many more places for perimetric changes (Fig. 62).

Fig. 62

Changes need not necessarily be equal throughout the length of the change. They may be made at one end of a line and tapered to nothing or very little at the other end (Fig. 63).

Fig. 63

Changes need not necessarily be made in pairs. For instance: You may add to the bodice-front side seam and not the bodice-back side seam (Fig. 64a). You may add to the back-sleeve seam but not the front-sleeve seam (Fig. 64b). You may add to the skirt-back seam but not the skirt-front seam (Fig. 64c). Make changes only where you need them.

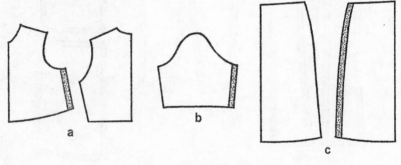

Fig. 64

However, you must make corresponding changes in pattern sections that join where a change affects the joining. For instance:

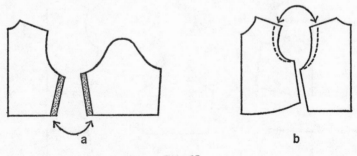

Fig. 65

If you add to the bodice-back side seam, you must add to the back-sleeve seam to provide a back-sleeve cap that will fit the changed back armhole (Fig. 65a).

If you narrow the bodice-front shoulder seam, you must also narrow the bodice-back shoulder seam to match (Fig. 65b).

Changes on Outside Lines Affect Length and Width. The easiest changes to make are over-all, balanced changes in length at the bottom of a unit.

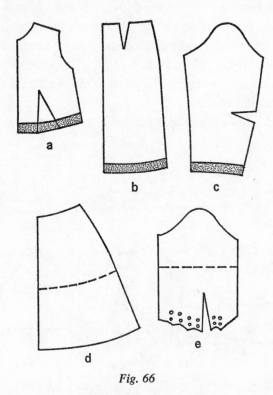

Fig. 66

Where there are no design details or where the change will not affect the amount of dart control, the change is truly simple (Figs. 66b and c). Where the change will affect the amount of dart control (Fig. 66a) or where there are design details (Figs. 66d and e), one must make a judgment as to the best place to make the change.

In Fig. 66a, the amount of dart control will be changed in addition to the length. If a changed dart is also required then the length adjustment does two things at once. If a dart change is not required, you have the choice of making your adjustment some other place or altering the dart control to fit after the length adjustment has been made.

In Fig. 66d, the amount of fullness is changed in addition to the length. When this is desirable—that is, a proportionate reduction or increase in fullness for a short or tall figure—do make it at the bottom. Should you wish to preserve the original fullness, make the change within the pattern.

In Fig. 66e, you have no choice. To shorten the pattern at the bottom would mean the elimination of the design detail. This change must be made within the pattern.

Patterns generally designate the place to make changes (the broken lines in Figs. 66d and e).

Length added to the top of a pattern also involves other considerations.

FOR EXAMPLE:

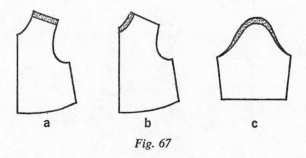

a   b   c

Fig. 67

Length may be added at the shoulder (Fig. 67a) but this will make both the neckline and the armhole larger.

A shoulder may be broadened at the neckline (Fig. 67b) but this will make the neckline smaller. Or, the neckline may be raised (Fig. 67b) but this will make the shoulder broader.

Length may be added to the sleeve cap (Fig. 67c) but will it fit the existing armhole?

In each case one must weigh the results of the change against one's figure needs. When a change is made in one pattern section be sure to make a corresponding change in the section that joins it.

GRADING RATHER THAN ABRUPT CHANGES

As a general rule it is safe to make changes up to ⅝ inch (a seam allowance) in any one place. A larger amount will distort the shape and style line of the pattern and move the darts out of position. It is wiser to alter the pattern proportionately, as in grading, by making small changes in several places. This may mean changes not only on the outside edges but within the pattern as well.

CHANGES WITHIN THE PATTERN

Changes within the pattern are made on the principle of slash and spread or its reverse, slash and overlap (or tuck). When the change is an equal one in width or in length across the entire pattern, it is called a *balanced change* (Figs. 68a and b). When the change is made in one place only, it is called a *change for circularity* (Figs. 68c and d).

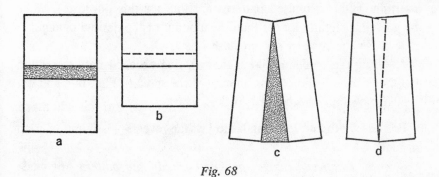

Fig. 68

To make the pattern larger for either balanced fullness or for circularity, *slash and spread* the pattern (Figs. 68a and c).

To make the pattern smaller for either balanced fullness or for circularity, *slash and overlap* or *tuck* (Figs. 68b and d).

To Make Balanced Changes—More Width or More Length

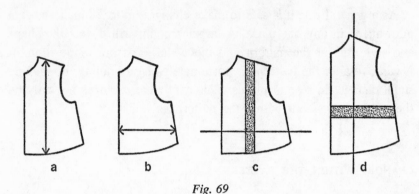

Fig. 69

1. Draw a slash line through the pattern. A vertical slash line is used for a change in width (Fig. 69a). This line is parallel to the grain line (if the grain line is long enough it may be used for this purpose). For a change in length, draw a horizontal slash line at right angles to the grain line (Fig. 69b).

2. Draw a similar guideline on the paper you plan to use for the insertion. (Old or unused patterns are fine for this purpose.) Make the guideline slightly longer than the amount of the desired change.

3. Slash the pattern on the slash line.

4. Using the guideline like a skewer, line up each pattern section and the paper insertion to the amount of the spread (Figs. 69c and d).

5. Scotch tape the pattern to the insertion.

For less width and less length, do just the reverse—slash and overlap or tuck.

Over-all balanced changes in length within the pattern are made only where needed. This may be above or below the bust (Fig. 70a), above or below the shoulder blades (Fig. 70b), above or below the elbow (Fig. 70d), above or below the hips (Fig. 70c). If necessary, changes may be made in both places (Fig. 70e and f).

Over-all balanced changes in width are also made only where they are needed—at the center front or back (Fig. 71a), the side seams—

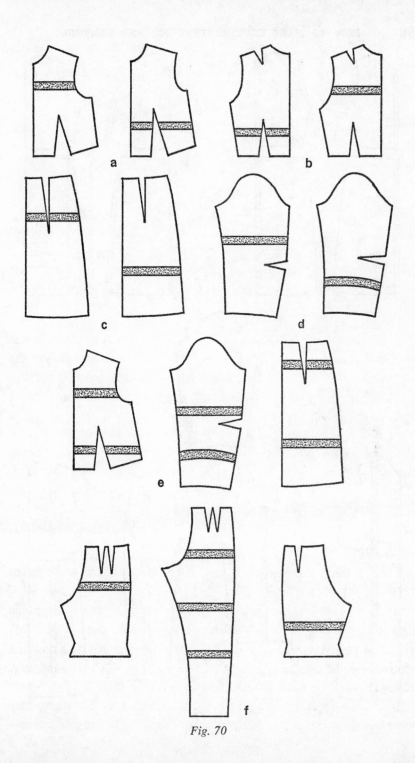

Fig. 70

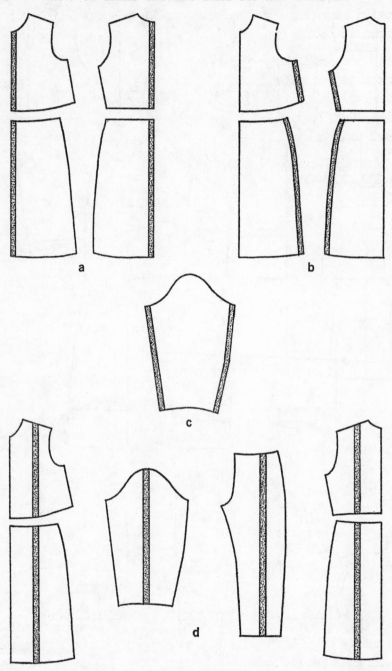

Fig. 71

front or back (Fig. 71b), the underarm sleeve seams (Fig. 71c), or within the pattern (Fig. 71d).

To Make Changes for Circularity (unequal changes)—There are several ways of making changes for circularity, that is, changes on *one edge only* while maintaining the original measurement at the other edge. Which method you choose depends on the kind of change that needs to be made.

METHOD I—*slash and spread or overlap* as if one were opening or shutting a fan.

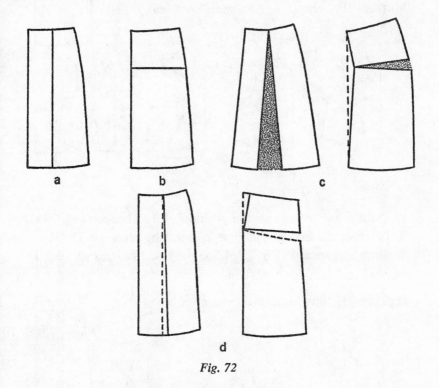

Fig. 72

1. Draw a vertical slash line parallel to the grain line for vertical circularity (Fig. 72a). Draw a horizontal slash line at right angles to the grain line for horizontal circularity (Fig. 72b). The slash line must extend the entire length or width of the pattern for this type of

change. If it stops short of the opposite side then the change must be made by Method II.

2. Slash on the slash line *to* but *not through* the edge to retain the original measurement. Spread to the desired amount for increased fullness (Fig. 72c) or slash and overlap (tuck) to decrease fullness (Fig. 72d).

3. Insert tissue in the spread area. In both types of change, Scotch tape to position.

Method I produces a change *throughout the pattern piece. Method II* limits the change to *one small area only.*

METHOD II—*changes in one small area only*

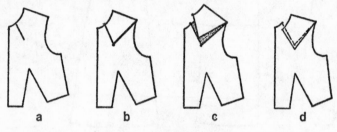

Fig. 73

1. Draw a line to indicate the position of the change (Fig. 73a).

2. Connect the end of this line to a nearby seam (Fig. 73b).

3. Slash and spread (Fig. 73c) for increased fullness or slash and overlap (Fig. 73d) for less fullness.

METHOD III—*involves the dart control*

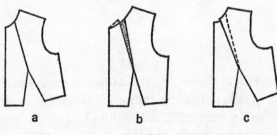

Fig. 74

This type of change should be used only when you really mean to *change the dart control,* too. For example—these neckline changes:

1. Draw a slash line from the point of contemplated change to the dart point (Fig. 74a).

2. Cut out the dart. Slash on the slash line to the dart point but not through it.

3. Using the dart point as a pivot, spread the pattern (Fig. 74b). This throws some of the dart control into the neckline. Note that as the neckline absorbs some of the dart control and becomes longer, the waistline dart becomes smaller.

OR

3. Using the dart point as a pivot, overlap the pattern at the neckline (Fig. 74c). This will make the neckline smaller but the dart larger. (This is the correction for a gaping neckline.)

Dart control doesn't ever just disappear. It is displaced; it must go somewhere else. Here is an example of how this works in a frequent adjustment for fit—excess length at the front armhole (Fig. 75a).

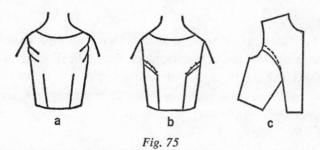

a   b   c

Fig. 75

The excess length is pinned out at the armhole to the dart point (Fig. 75b) thereby creating a bulge in the pattern. To flatten the pattern (the only way in which it can be used) cut out the dart. You will find that the dart control which was pinned out at the armhole reappears in the waistline dart enlarging it (Fig. 75c).

METHOD IV—*variation of the circularity change that involves a dart*
The following illustration is for a bodice front. Changes are made in exactly the same way on any other pattern sections.

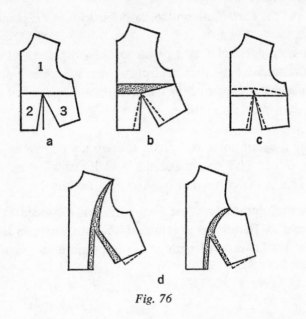

Fig. 76

1. Draw a slash line across the bodice front and through the waist-line dart parallel to the center front or the vertical grain line (Fig. 76a). Label sections 1, 2, and 3 as illustrated.

2. Slash and spread—equally to the dart point between sections 1 and 2, tapering from the dart point to the side seam between sections 1 and 3 (Fig. 76b).

3. Relocate the dart point in the center of the spread area. Draw new dart legs of equal length (Fig. 76b). The size of the new dart is determined by the shaping need.

This method of handling a correction has the merit of preserving the center-front line. Incidentally, this is a good correction for a full-bosomed figure that requires more length at the center front only and more shaping.

The reverse of this (shortened center-front line and smaller dart) is the correction for a flat or hollow-chested figure. Directions for this change follow.

1. Draw slash lines across the bodice front and through the waist-line, dart parallel to the center front. Label sections 1, 2, and 3 (Fig. 76a).

2. Slash and overlap—an equal amount between sections 1 and 2 to the dart point, tapering from the dart point to the side seam between sections 1 and 3 (Fig. 76c).

3. Relocate the dart as directed above (Fig. 76b).

Ease across the bust and across the shoulder blades can be added by Method IV (Fig. 76d).

Draw a slash line from the shoulder when more ease is desired across the chest or across the back as well as through the bust and shoulder blades.

Draw a slash line from the armhole when more ease is desired only through the bust or shoulder blades while preserving a satisfactory fit across the chest and across the back.

Relocate the dart point in the center of the spread area. Draw new dart legs of equal length.

A Word of Caution About Changes for Circularity. Remember that *a pattern is flat and should remain so,* no matter what the pattern change. Slash lines may originate on any outside line but they *must terminate at some seam line or dart*. Were they to stop short of these terminal points (Fig. 77a) the result would be a bulge when the pattern is overlapped (Fig. 77b) or bunching where the pattern is strained by the spread (Fig. 77c). In this condition the pattern cannot be used for cutting out material.

a   b   c

Fig. 77

Pattern Changes for Length as Well as Width—Balanced as Well as in One Place Only. If pattern changes were simple, fitting would be easy. Many figures require complex changes. A bulge or full curve requires length to get over it as well as width to get around it. This is the pattern change for one who has a full bust, a heavy arm, a prominent seat or abdomen. To further complicate matters the change may

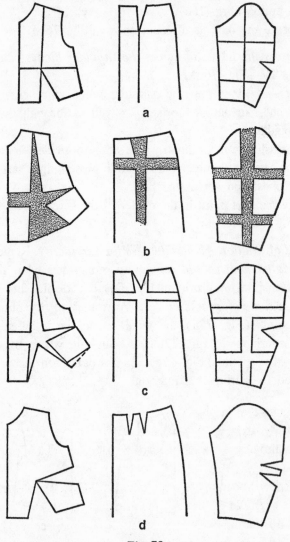

Fig. 78

be equal in one part and unequal in another. Fig. 78 presents a few such fitting problems and a method for solving them.

1. Draw a vertical as well as a horizontal slash line (Fig. 78a).

2. Slash and spread in both directions. This may be a balanced change, a change for circularity, or both depending on the need (Fig. 78b).

3. Relocate the dart when necessary (Fig. 78c). If the change results in too much dart control for one dart, divide the control into two darts or make multiple darts (Fig. 78d).

METHOD V—*cut-on or cut-off*

There is yet another way of making pattern changes. You may simply *cut-on* or *cut-off* your correction. This presupposes that you know what the correction is and that you are familiar with the shape and amount of the change. This last method is a kind of reward for having worked out your problems the hard way first.

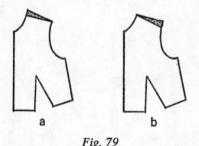

Fig. 79

FOR INSTANCE:

If you know you must always build up the shoulder at the front neckline by ½ inch to take care of a thicker-than-standard base of the neck, simply *cut-on* this amount as you cut out the pattern (Fig. 79a).

If you know you must always take off ½ inch of your shoulder seam at the armhole to provide the angle for your sloping shoulders, simply *cut-off* this amount as you cut out the pattern (Fig. 79b).

And so on with any other changes you may know so well.

PATTERN CORRECTIONS

Sometimes when a pattern is slashed and spread (Figs. 80a and b) or slashed and overlapped (Fig. 80c and d) it is thrown out of kilter.

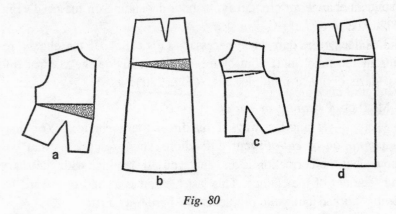

Fig. 80

This calls for a correction (Fig. 81).

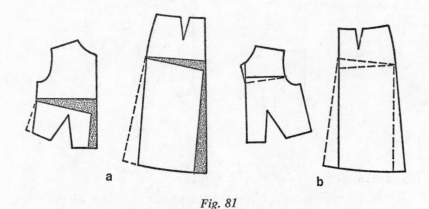

Fig. 81

The shaded areas in Fig. 81a are amounts that have been added.

1. Extend the center-front lines to establish the new center fronts (shaded area—Fig. 81a).

2. Subtract from the jutting area the amount just added to the front (broken lines in Fig. 81a) to balance the measurement.

OR

The jutting lines at the center fronts in Fig. 81b are the result of the slash and overlap.

1. Extend the center-front lines to establish the new center fronts (solid lines in Fig. 81b).

2. Add to the other side an amount equal to what was subtracted at the center fronts (solid lines in Fig. 81b).

Whenever an undefined space results from a slash and spread (Fig. 82a) new lines must be drawn on each side to connect the ends of the broken lines (Fig. 82b). In the case of a long, curved line, a more accurate guide is achieved by drawing several slash lines instead of one (Fig. 82c), slashing and spreading all of them (Fig. 82d).

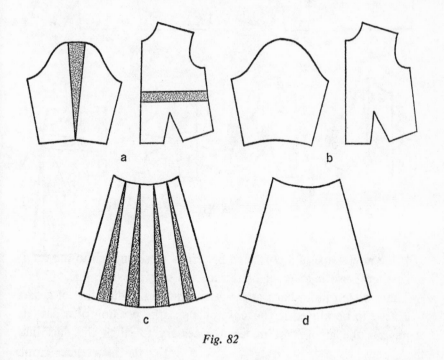

a   b

c   d

Fig. 82

Whenever a jagged line results from an overlapping or tucking of the pattern (Fig. 83a) a new line must be drawn to correct the protruding pattern (Fig. 83b). The new line begins at the point where it originally began and goes to the point at which it originally ended, cutting off all projecting edges (Fig. 83c). A jagged grain line is corrected in the same way.

There are many times when the process of shifting one section to meet another will produce an angular joining where it is not desirable. This can be corrected with a smoothly curved line drawn freehand or with any of your curved instruments (Fig. 83d).

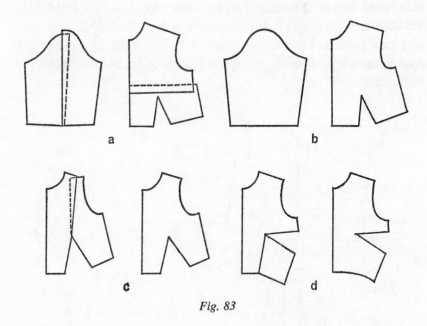

Fig. 83

If the new shape of a corrected pattern is close enough to the original pattern, use it to recut or retrace the original style line.

That pointed little shape at the seam line and cutting line of a dart will need to be moved if you have changed the position of a dart. It represents the amount of material necessary to stitch the dart into the seam.

1. Fold the dart closed as if for stitching and to that position in which it will be pressed. The rule for pressing darts is as follows: horizontal darts are pressed down, vertical darts are pressed toward

the center. All of this is on the wrong side, of course. The folding will produce a bulging pattern.

2. Holding the dart in the position described above, cut along the cutting line.

3. Unfold the dart.

THE RIGHT TOOL MAKES LIFE EASIER

When the correction has produced a shape different from the original pattern, a new line must be supplied—straight or curved as needed. Straight lines are always drawn with a ruler or yardstick. Curved lines may be drawn freehand first, then "trued up" with the appropriate drafting instrument. Or, they may be drawn directly with the drafting instrument.

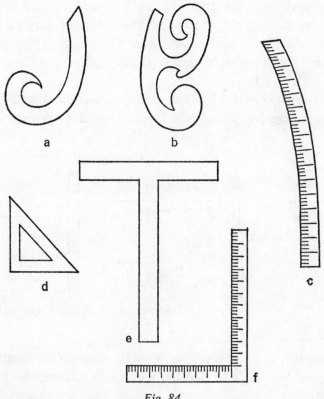

Fig. 84

You are, in truth, redrafting your pattern by the changes you are making. You will find the work very much easier by the use of the proper drafting tools.

For curved lines there are a number of transparent curves designated by number. Two of the most useful for home patternmakers are Dietzgen No. 17, the armscye (Fig. 84a), used to create the armhole, the neckline, and any similar curves and Dietzgen No. 16, a somewhat flattened series of curves used wherever any of its lines seem appropriate (Fig. 84b).

There is also a curved ruler (sometimes called a curved stick) (Fig. 84c) for longer curved lines, for example: the side seam of a skirt, a curved style line, or control seam.

In using any of the above curved instruments, it is not necessary to use the entire curve at one time, though there will be times when you may want to do so. Simply slide the curved instrument along until you find that part of it that approximates the curve of your corrected pattern. Use as much of it as you need to complete or correct a line.

For establishing a right angle use a 45° triangle (Fig. 84d), a T square (Fig. 84e), or a tailor's square (sometimes called an L square) (Fig. 84f).

To draw a right angle (Fig. 85) place your instrument with the 90° angle against the line you wish to "square" and draw the new line.

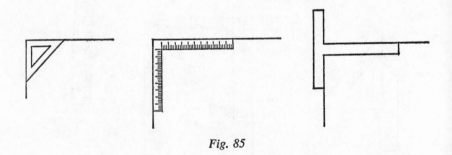

Fig. 85

Incidentally, the hypotenuse of the 45° triangle (the slanting line opposite the 90° angle or "square") will give you the bias grain of the fabric.

All of the above instruments may be purchased at an artists' supply store or any other place where they would be likely to sell drafting tools. Sometimes dressmaker's and tailor's supply stores also carry them.

No One Way

When dealing with any art form, one must recognize the fact that there is no one right way to do anything. *What works is right; what doesn't is wrong.* Some methods may be preferable to others only because they may bring results a little easier, perhaps faster, and more certainly.

So it is with fitting. There is no one way for making a pattern change. There is a choice of methods. Which you choose may depend as much on the design and the fabric as on your figure needs. Following are some suggestions for handling some frequent fitting problems.

Correction for

THICK NECK

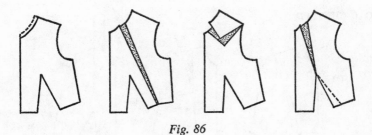

Fig. 86

THIN NECK — reverse the procedure

BROAD SHOULDERS

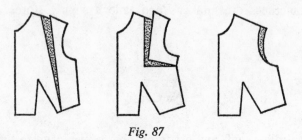

Fig. 87

NARROW SHOULDERS — reverse the procedure

SQUARE SHOULDERS

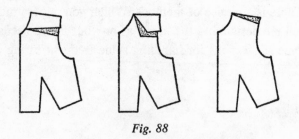

Fig. 88

SLOPING SHOULDERS — reverse the procedure

BROAD-CHESTED

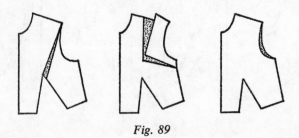

Fig. 89

NARROW-CHESTED—reverse the procedure

LARGE-BOSOMED

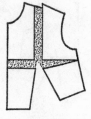

Fig. 90

FLAT-CHESTED — reverse the procedure

HOLLOW CHESTED

Fig. 91

HIGH BUST

Fig. 92

LOW BUST — reverse the procedure

LONG-WAISTED

Fig. 93

SMALL-WAISTED — reverse the procedure

THICK WAIST

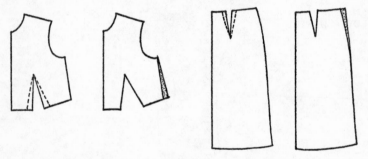

Fig. 94

SMALL WAIST — reverse the procedure

ROUNDED BACK

Fig. 95

STRAIGHT BACK — reverse the procedure

BROAD BACK

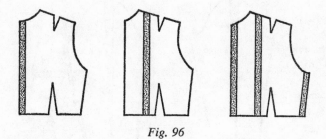

Fig. 96

NARROW BACK — reverse the procedure

PROMINENT SHOULDER BLADES

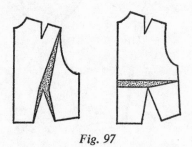

Fig. 97

TIGHT ARMHOLE

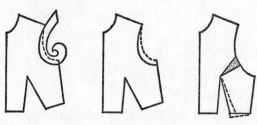

Fig. 98

SAGGING ARMHOLE — reverse the procedure

HEAVY UPPER ARM

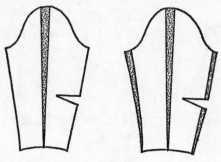

Fig. 99

SLIM UPPER ARM — reverse the procedure

MUSCULAR UPPER ARM

Fig. 100

SLEEVE STRAIN ACROSS UPPER ARM

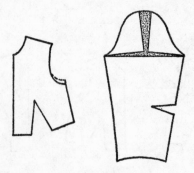

Fig. 101

SLEEVE CAP TOO BIG — reverse the procedure

SLEEVE CAP TOO SHORT

Fig. 102

SLEEVE CAP TOO LONG — reverse the procedure

MORE MOVEMENT

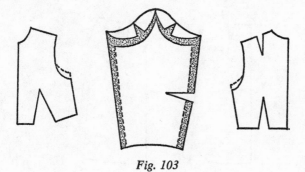

Fig. 103

MORE ELBOW ROOM

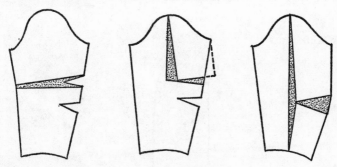

Fig. 104

LESS ELBOW ROOM — reverse the procedure

WIDER WRIST

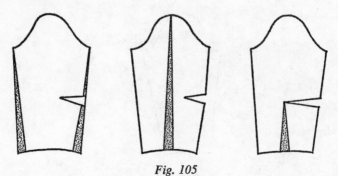

Fig. 105

NARROWER WRIST — reverse the procedure

BIG-HIPPED

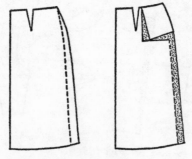

Fig. 106

SLIM-HIPPED — reverse the procedure

SWAYBACKED

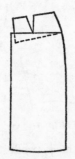

Fig. 107

PROMINENT SEAT OR PROMINENT ABDOMEN

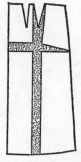

Fig. 108

FLAT REAR OR FLAT ABDOMEN — reverse the procedure

SKIRT CUPS UNDER BUTTOCKS

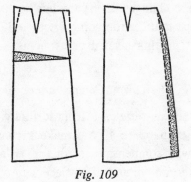

Fig. 109

HEAVY THIGHS

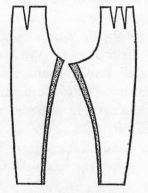

Fig. 110

SLIM THIGHS—reverse the procedure

LARGE SEAT

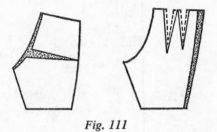

Fig. 111

FLAT SEAT — reverse the procedure

Obviously we have not exhausted the scope of figure vagaries or the possibilities of pattern changes. Everyone has her own little problem. It is the author's hope that the foregoing discussion does provide some theoretical basis for making needed adjustments.

The Law of Compensation

Patterns are like jigsaw puzzles. All those funny little shapes must fit right up against each other. If you make a change in one piece, you must in some way compensate for this in an adjoining piece.

There may be a certain amount of displacement within a given area. Seams or darts may be relocated within a given area while the over-all measurement remains the same. For instance:

If you lower a waistline, a corresponding amount is taken off the top of the skirt. If you raise a waistline, a corresponding amount is taken off the lower portion of the bodice.

When a shoulder seam is moved forward, some may be taken off the front but that amount is added to the back.

When the side seam of a skirt is repositioned, what is taken off the front is added to the back and vice versa.

When an armhole seam is moved in to narrow a shoulder, it may be necessary to lengthen the sleeve cap in order to preserve the proper placement of the grain.

If a dart is made larger, a corresponding amount should be added to the side seam. When a dart is made smaller, a corresponding amount may be taken off the side seam.

The "Whole" Truth

No one is perfectly symmetrical. The right side of your face is different from the left side; so are the right side and left side of your body. You may have one higher shoulder or one higher hip. Everyone has some variation between right and left sides. What, then, does one do about altering a pattern which generally comes in halves, and from which one cuts both sides alike?

For most people the variations are not so great as to call for two separate sets of adjustments—one for each side. You can see how that would complicate your cutting. It is much simpler to settle for one pattern that fits the larger side and provides enough material to cover your greatest needs. The smaller side can then be fitted out on the figure. The excess cloth can be trimmed away.

If your fitting problem is this very thing—great discrepancy between right and left sides—then *do* make two patterns and cut each side separately. It's a lot more work but it may be the answer to your problem.

Not only are right and left sides often different but there may be two completely different types of pattern alterations for front and back. Visualize, if you will, a heavy-bosomed, erect figure. The pattern correction for this figure calls for lengthening and widening the front bodice and shortening and narrowing the back bodice—two opposite procedures.

Once one gets past the frustration of not knowing what to do to make the pattern fit, the whole subject of pattern alteration becomes a very fascinating one. No two people are alike. To fit each is a challenge.

Good fit starts with the pattern; it doesn't end there. What a properly adjusted pattern can do is to eliminate the worst pitfalls before cutting so that you have something to work with in the fabric. If measurements alone could guarantee good fit, how easy it would all be!

Chapter V

FIT THAT FLATTERS

HOW TO MAKE THE FABRIC FIT THE FIGURE

Your first reaction on looking at a costume may be of delight in or dismay at its fit. When you begin to analyze *why* you become aware of the size, the ease, the grain, the shaping, the silhouette seams. All of these are interrelated but for purposes of study we shall examine them separately. This is not always easy to do. One can no more make a diagnosis of what's wrong with the fit of a garment on an isolated symptom than one can in diagnosing a headache. The headache may be due to your eyes, your ears, your nose, your stomach or only to the fact that your mother-in-law is arriving for dinner. A wrinkle in a dress may be caused by insufficient or excessive length, insufficient or excessive width, insufficient or excessive dart control. It is necessary to check out all the symptoms to determine which is the offender. What's more, in correcting one, you will undoubtedly be affecting the others.

Fit Is an Integral Part of Current Style

While there are certain objective elements by which good fit can be judged, that *judgment must be made within the context of at-this-moment-in-this-place fashion*. If, at that moment, in that part of the globe, fashion is preoccupied with bosoms and buttocks, to wear an easy-fitting shift dress makes a gal look as if she had just emerged from some hinterland out of touch with the contemporary world. If, however, shifts are all the rage, then a skintight dress that reveals a bulging bosom and a billowy bottom makes one look like a leftover of another era. *Fit is an integral part of a current style.*

Fitting for Size and Ease

We have dealt with the matter of size and ease at some length in Chapter I. It may bear rereading at this time.

BRIEFLY—TO REFRESH YOUR MEMORY

Size is determined by body measurements and figure type. Ease is an amount added to body measurements in order to provide clothes with enough room to make them comfortable and sufficient cloth to conceal figure faults.

The amount of ease depends on the design of the garment, its function, and your own personal preference.

Commercial patterns include ease; you do not need to add any unless fitting indicates that more is needed.

It is easier and wiser to alter the pattern rather than the garment. In the fitting stage about all one can do is raise as much as possible, drop as much as possible, take in as much as possible, let out as much as possible—and hope for the best! Look to whatever seams and darts are available for even tiny changes. One eighth of an inch on a seam may not seem very much but multiply that by the number of seams and you may be surprised to find how much this adds up to. Every little bit helps.

It is very disheartening to send a garment precisely fitted for size and ease to the cleaners only to have it returned a size smaller. To prevent such disaster make certain that everything that goes into the making of your garment—inside and out—has been sponged or preshrunk. Labeling will indicate when this has been done at the factory (most factories do treat fabric for shrinkage before distribution). If you are in doubt, treat the fabric yourself. Either sponge it (woolens), immerse it in cold water (linens and cottons), or have it dry cleaned (silks and precious cottons and linens).

In early fittings, be mindful of the fact that the garment is yet to get interfacing, underlining, facing, lining—perhaps even an interlining. All of these make the garment fit a little more snugly when completed.

MINIMUM EASE FOR A BASIC-FITTED DRESS, JACKET, COAT

Fig. 112

Because coats and jackets are worn over other garments they must have additional ease (see page 11 for basic-fitting dress ease). The broken lines in Figs. 112b and c indicate the original basic-fitting dress pattern.

How to Make the Basic-fitting Suit or Ensemble Jacket Pattern (Fig. 112b)

1. Start with the basic-fitting dress pattern. Make all changes— front and back—from this.
2. Drop the neckline ⅛ inch.
3. Add ¼ inch ease to the side seams. This makes the basic-fitting jacket have 1 inch more ease than the basic-fitting dress.
4. Broaden the shoulders ½ inch.
5. Lower the armhole ½ inch.

How to Make the Basic-fitting Coat Pattern (Fig. 112c)

1. Start with the basic-fitting dress pattern. Make all changes front and back—from this.
2. Drop the neckline ¼ inch.
3. Add ½ inch ease to the side seams. This makes the basic-fitting coat have 2 inches more ease than the basic-fitting dress.
4. Broaden the shoulders ½ inch.
5. Lower the armhole 1 inch.

Note that in both the jacket and coat patterns, the neckline has been lowered, the shoulders widened, the armhole dropped, and width has been added across the chest, across the back, and at the side seams. Corresponding changes are made in the jacket and coat sleeves. The sleeve cap is flattened and widened to fit the extended shoulder and the deepened armhole. The underarm seam is lengthened to compensate for the flattened cap. The wrist is widened.

The Basic-fitting Dress, Jacket, and Coat Sleeve* (Fig. 113)

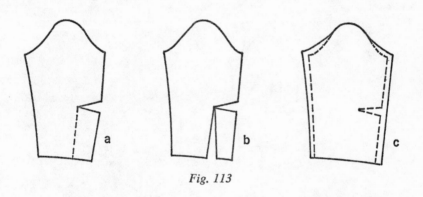

Fig. 113

How to Make the One-piece Jacket Sleeve (Fig. 113)

1. Start with the one-piece dress sleeve (Fig. 113a).

2. Shift some of the elbow dart control to the wrist to widen it (Figs. 113a and b). Leave the wrist dart control unstitched for fullness.

3. Add ¼ inch ease to the side seams (Fig. 113c).

4. Raise the underarm curve ½ inch (Fig. 113c). (See page 109 for directions.)

5. Redraw the sleeve cap. Compare the length of the cap with the jacket armhole. Allow 1½–2 inches ease. (The original dress sleeve cap has 1 to 1½ inches ease.) The solid lines in Fig. 113c represent the new sleeve.

* The common two-piece dress, jacket, or coat sleeve is a style variation of the one-piece sleeve.

How to Make the One-piece Coat Sleeve (Fig. 113)

Steps 1 and 2 are the same as for the jacket sleeve.

3. Add 1 inch ease to the side seams (Fig. 113c).

4. Raise the underarm curve 1 inch (Fig. 113c).

5. Redraw the sleeve cap. Compare the length of the new sleeve cap with the coat armhole. Allow 1½–2 inches ease.

HOW TO COMPARE THE SLEEVE CAP WITH THE ARMHOLE (Fig. 114)

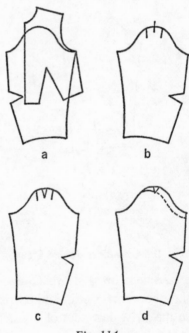

a   b

c   d

Fig. 114

1. Start at the underarm seam and match the underarm curve of the sleeve with the underarm curve of the armhole (Fig. 114a).

2. Using a pin for a pivot continue to match a tiny section at a time (about ⅛ inch) of sleeve and armhole from the underarm to the shoulder.

3. Mark the place where the shoulder of the bodice appears on the sleeve cap.

4. Do the same for the other side. You will find a space between the two marks (Fig. 114b). This leftover space is the ease.

5. Place the shoulder notch of the sleeve cap at the center of the space dividing the ease equally between front and back (Fig. 114c).

NOTE: the notch should be at the crest of the curve. If it isn't, re-draw the curve so that it will be (Fig. 114d). This will assure that the back sleeve cap will fit the back armhole and the front sleeve cap, the front armhole.

If the comparison of sleeve cap and armhole reveals too much ease, lower or narrow the cap, depending on your build. If the comparison reveals not enough ease, raise or widen the sleeve cap depending on build. The only way to tell if the correction yields the right amount of ease is to test the sleeve cap in the armhole once more.

Just-right Ease

When a garment fits right for size and ease it is neither too loose nor too tight. It is not flapping about like a scarecrow nor is it popping your buttons. There is sufficient room to walk, to sit, to bend, to move within the purpose for which the dress or suit or coat was designed.

To make certain that clothes have the correct amount of ease in the needed places, fit from the skin out—first you, then your foundation garment, then the garment. Fit a jacket over the skirt, blouse, or dress to be worn with it. Fit a coat over the dress, suit, skirt, sweater, or blouse you intend to wear with it.

You should be able to swish the skirt easily around the hips when standing and be comfortable when seated—even if the skirt has a snug-fitting waist and closely fitted hips. In a garment with fitted, set-in sleeves you should be able to move the arms forward within reason, though it isn't necessary to test a street dress as if you were swinging a baseball bat. That fold of fabric that appears at the front armhole (the back armhole, too) is necessary. Were you to fit it out of exist-ence, you would eliminate the movement it provides. You cannot have an absolutely smooth fit at this place and movement, too.

If you constantly have to yank your clothes into position because they are riding up or if you must clutch them to disguise their bigness, or if you immobilize yourself for fear of breaking out at the seams, your chances for enjoying whatever it is that you are doing are completely ruined. You will feel self-conscious and unattractive. Therefore, you will not look attractive. Size and ease of movement must be given priority in any consideration of fit.

Fluctuating weight presents a size-and-ease problem for many women who "puff up" periodically. In truth, the gain or loss of a pound or two doesn't appreciably affect the fit of a garment. Nothing should fit so tight that it would. Should this on-again, off-again weight differential make your clothes uncomfortable, try nylon tape closures, elastic strips in the side waistband or drawstrings to tide you over your heavy periods. Better yet, choose easy-fitting styles.

Unless a dress is designed like a maternity dress, no style can absorb a large change in weight—up or down. Changes on side seams are only a small part of the needed change. Far more serious is the necessary change in shaping. This can only be accomplished by recutting and remaking the entire garment.

Rescue Operations for Size and Ease

In the following section, the "a" figures illustrate the problem, the "b" figures—the rescue operation, the "c" figures—hindsight, or pattern changes that would have prevented the dilemma. (See the previous chapter for complete directions.) Notice how often the lack of a simple pattern alteration can become an involved fitting operation.

Help comes from two natural allies—the fabric and your hands. Let the fabric tell you where it wants to go. This is often your best clue as to what needs doing. Then let your hands take over. Learn to use them to smooth the material over the body until the fabric eases into a correct position. Learn to "pinch out" any excess cloth.

Many a sewer can solve her fitting problems abstractly but many more think with their hands.

How to Deal with Folds and Wrinkles Due to Excess Length

ACROSS THE SHOULDERS, ACROSS THE CHEST OR BACK (Fig. 115a).

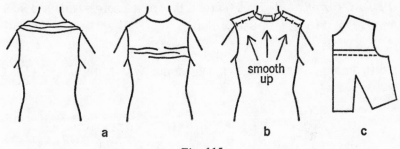

Fig. 115

Fitting: Release the shoulder, armhole, and side seam (when necessary). Smooth the fabric toward the shoulders and armhole. Clip the neckline until the fabric lies smoothly at the base of the neck. Refit and repin the shoulder seam. Trim away the excess fabric. Recut the neckline and the armhole from the original pattern (Fig. 115b).

Pattern Correction: Tuck the pattern across the chest or across the back (Fig. 115c).

ACROSS THE BUST, ACROSS THE SHOULDER BLADES (Fig. 116a)

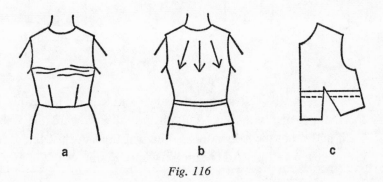

Fig. 116

Fitting: Release the side seams as far as necessary. Let the lower part of the bodice drop over the waistline. Refit and repin the side seams to the waistline. Adjust the darts. Establish a new waistline (see page 106). Add seam allowance. Trim away the excess length (Fig. 116b). If the bodice fits well from bust to waist, make the corrections from bust to shoulders as directed in Fig. 115.

Pattern Correction: Tuck across the bust, across the shoulder blades (Fig. 116c). Adjust the darts.

AT THE BODICE WAISTLINE, AT THE SKIRT WAISTLINE (Fig. 117a)

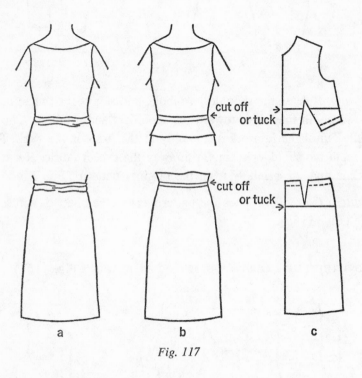

cut off
or tuck

cut off
or tuck

a   b   c

Fig. 117

Fitting: Release the side seams of bodice and skirt as far as necessary to eliminate the wrinkling. Smooth the fabric toward the waistline. Refit and repin the side seams to the waistline. Adjust the darts. Establish a new waistline. Add seam allowance. Trim away the excess material (Fig. 117b).

Pattern Correction: Either trim away the excess length at the waistline or tuck the pattern (Fig. 117c). Adjust the darts.

AT THE HIPS (Fig. 118a)

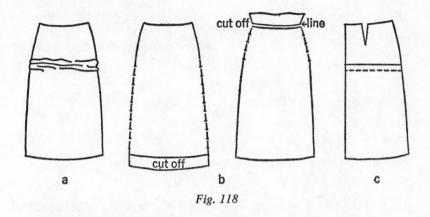

Fig. 118

Fitting: If the waist-to-hip area fits well, release the side seams below the hips. Repin. Adjust the length at the hem. If the waist-to-hip area needs adjustment, release the side seams from the hips up. Refit and repin. Adjust the darts. Establish a new waistline (Fig. 118b).

Pattern Correction: Tuck at the hipline (Fig. 118c).

IN THE SLEEVE: ABOVE THE ELBOW (Fig. 119a), BELOW THE ELBOW (Fig. 119b)

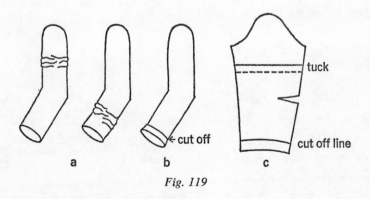

Fig. 119

Fitting: Above the elbow: release the underarm seam. Refit and repin. Relocate the elbow dart. Trim away the extra length at the wrist.

Below the elbow: simply trim away the extra length at the wrist (Fig. 119b).

Pattern Correction: Above the elbow: tuck the pattern, below the elbow: cut off at the wrist (Fig. 119c).

Wrinkling, Pulling, Straining, Binding Due to Insufficient Width

ACROSS THE SHOULDERS AND NECKLINE (Fig. 120a)

If the muslin fitting reveals any of the above, slash at the point of strain and insert a wedge or strip of muslin.

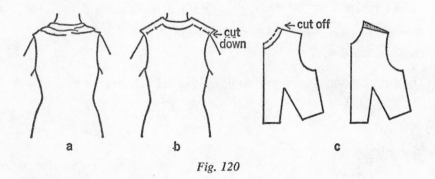

a   b   c

Fig. 120

Fitting: Release the shoulder seams. Smooth the fabric toward the shoulders, neckline, and armholes. Enlarge the neckline. Refit and repin the shoulder seams using as much of the seam allowance as possible (Fig. 120b).

Pattern Correction: Enlarge the neckline and/or build up the shoulders at the neckline (Fig. 120c).

ACROSS THE CHEST, ACROSS THE BACK (Fig. 121a)

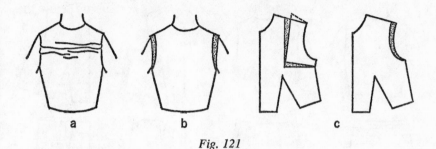

Fig. 121

Fitting: Add ease at the armhole by using as much of any seam allowances as possible (Fig. 121b).

Pattern Correction: Slash and spread for extra width (Fig. 121c). Cut-on extra width at the armhole.

ACROSS THE BUST, ACROSS THE SHOULDER BLADES (Fig. 122a)

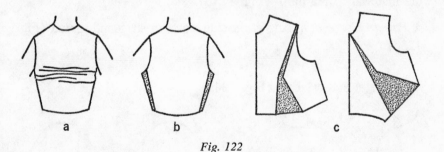

Fig. 122

Fitting: Release the side seams. Add width by using as much of the seam allowances as possible. If the dart extends to the bust point, lower it, releasing a bit more material (Fig. 122b).

Pattern Correction: Slash and spread for additional ease (Fig. 122c). Relocate the dart in the spread area.

AT THE WAISTLINE—BODICE AND/OR SKIRT (Fig. 123a)

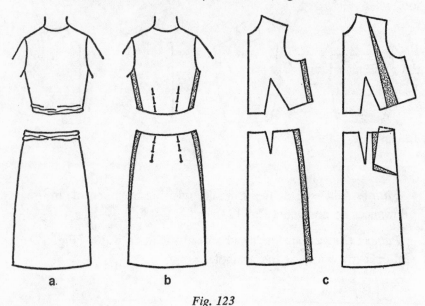

a   b   c

Fig. 123

Fitting: Release the side seams. Unpin the darts. Add width by using some of the side seam allowances and when possible some of the material in the darts (Fig. 123b).

Pattern Correction: Add at the side seams or slash and spread (Fig. 123c).

ACROSS THE SLEEVE CAP (Fig. 124a)

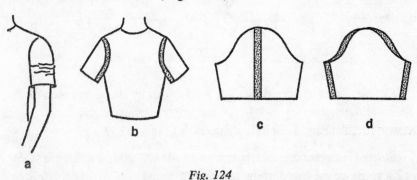

a   b   c   d

Fig. 124

Fitting: Unpin the sleeve. Use some of the seam allowances of the armhole and the sleeve cap for more width. Use the underarm seams, too, when necessary (Fig. 124b).

Pattern Correction: Slash and spread for additional width (Fig. 124c) or redraw the cap using the armscye (Fig. 124d) or cut on the required width.

ACROSS THE SLEEVE AND TIGHT ARMHOLE (Fig. 125a)

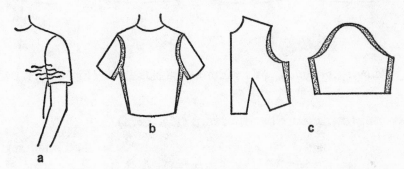

Fig. 125

Fitting: Drop the armhole, add width at both the armhole and the sleeve cap by using some of the seam allowances. Use some of the underarm seam allowance of the sleeve and the side seam of the bodice (Fig. 125b).

Pattern Correction: Add width to the armhole, sleeve cap, side seam of bodice and underarm seam of sleeve (Fig. 125c).

AT THE HIPS (Fig. 126a)

Fitting: Release the side seams. Refit and repin adding width by using some of the seam allowances. If the darts are involved, shorten them, releasing more material at the hips. If the skirt has sufficient length, it can be raised at the hips to fit, in which case the hip-to-waist area would need to be recut with additional width (Fig. 126b).

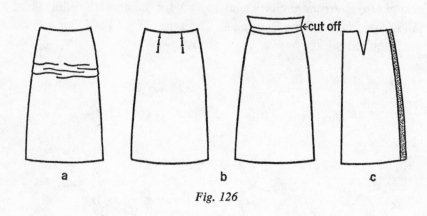

Fig. 126

Pattern Correction: Add width at the side seam (Fig. 126c).

AT THE LOWER PART OF THE SKIRT (Fig. 127a)

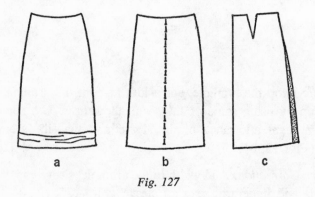

Fig. 127

Fitting: Release the side seams. Check the dart control. Let the material fall naturally with the grain. Refit and repin the side seams adding or subtracting to front and/or back as necessary (Fig. 127b).

Pattern Correction: Add or subtract to the front and/or back side seams (Fig. 127c).

If the Pattern Is Too Large or Too Wide or Too Long at any of the above places, it may be corrected by doing just the reverse of the suggested procedure. Pin out the fabric to fit. Determine the necessary change. Correct the pattern to match the needed change. Recut the fabric from the adjusted pattern.

In the fitting stage, it is certainly easier to make the garment smaller by cutting it away than to make it larger by adding fractions of the seam allowance. This is what tempts so many sewers to cut larger than the pattern. Cutting larger has its hazards, too, but it can be handled more easily. As a matter of fact if you have any doubts about the fit, it is wise to cut generous seam allowances so that you have something to work with should an adjustment need to be made. Expensive ready-to-wear is often cut this way to provide opportunities for adding length and width.

"HIKING UP," "POKING OUT" DUE TO INSUFFICIENT LENGTH OF BODICE (Fig. 128a)

(Note: this may also be due to insufficient dart control—see page 137)

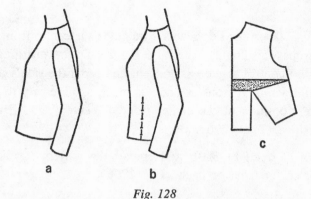

Fig. 128

Fitting: Release the shoulder seams and side seams. Straighten the center front or back or any other "pokes," dropping the waistline as necessary. Check the dart control. Add length by using as much as possible of the seam allowances at the shoulder, neck, and waistline.

Refit and repin all silhouette seams. Establish a new waistline (Fig. 128b).

Pattern Correction: Slash and spread pattern for additional length (Fig. 128c).

INSUFFICIENT LENGTH OF SKIRT (Fig. 129a)

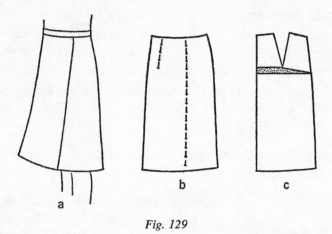

Fig. 129

Fitting: Release the side seams. Straighten the center front or back dropping the waistline as necessary. Fit the hip-to-waist area adjusting the dart control as necessary. Refit and repin the side seams adding or subtracting at front or back as much as necessary to preserve the correct position of the center front or center back. Establish a new waistline (Fig. 129b).

Pattern Correction: Slash and spread the pattern for additional length at center front or back (Fig. 129c).

INSUFFICIENT LENGTH OF SLEEVE CAP (Fig. 130)

Fitting: Release the armhole seam. Reset the sleeve using the horizontal grain as a guide. Use as much seam allowance as you can salvage at the cap of the sleeve (Fig. 130b).

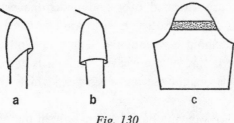

Fig. 130

Pattern Correction: Add length to the sleeve cap (Fig. 130c).

If the garment "caves in" at any of the above places instead of poking out, the correction is the reverse procedure. Remove the excess length.

Have you observed how many times in making a correction for length or width the grain, the dart control, and the silhouette seams are also involved. That's the way it is in fitting. All are closely interrelated.

Grain as a Guide

All fabrics, and therefore all garments, *hang with the grain.* In fact, they persist in hanging with the grain whether you cut them so or not. This often creates an unhappy effect you hadn't planned on or anticipated.

Grain makes all the difference between a garment that hangs right and one that doesn't. It is the best indicator that all is well or that something is wrong. So necessary to the appearance and hang of the garment is the grain that a wise sewer learns very early in her sewing career that she must always establish the grain before cutting the fabric, cut with the grain, stay stitch to preserve the grain, sew with the grain, press with the grain, and fit with the grain.

Perhaps you know the grain by another name. The patterns refer to it as "Straight of Goods." By whatever name, it is of the utmost importance to the success of the garment.

In principle, weaving is the same today as when man first began to weave cloth. One set of lengthwise yarns (warp) are placed side by side in a row on a loom. Another set of crosswise yarns (filler, woof, weft, or picks) are threaded over and under the warp yarns. The lengthwise yarns and the crosswise yarns are interlaced at right angles to each other, forming a rectangular length of cloth. Whatever the variations in the design of the weave, all cloth is woven in this way. It is these threads—lengthwise and crosswise—which are the grain of the fabric.

The advances in weaving have been mainly in the method of separating or lifting groups of yarns in the pattern of the weave so that the filling yarn can be inserted with one motion of a shuttle. Because they must withstand this separating and lifting, the warp yarns are set taut in the loom. Often they are even made of stronger threads. Because of this, fabrics hang best with the lengthwise grain and most fabrics are used in this way (Fig. 131a).

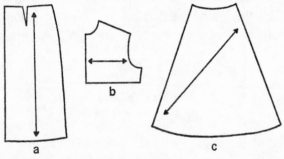

Fig. 131

Sometimes for a special effect a garment is cut in whole or in part on the horizontal grain (Fig. 131b). Or, both for decorative reasons and for a special kind of fit, fabric is used on the bias (Fig. 131c). Bias is stretchable and produces a molded, clinging, form-defining fit.

While most fabrics are meant to be used on the vertical grain, for many it makes little difference whether they are used on the vertical or horizontal grain. What is important is to maintain the right-angular position of the yarns.

Sometimes in the finishing process, the fabric is pulled off-grain. And sometimes, in cutting the yardage from the bolt, the cut edge is off-grain. The first thing the sewer must do before she can cut the garment is to restore the true grain so that the pattern may be accurately placed on the cloth.

Fitting with the Grain

Use any prominent lengthwise or crosswise yarn to help locate the grain. The straight line of any stripe, plaid, or check will serve in the same way. When the grain is too difficult to see at a glance, place a line of hand- or machine-guide basting to mark it. If you use hand-basting (often preferable) put the long floats of thread on the right side.

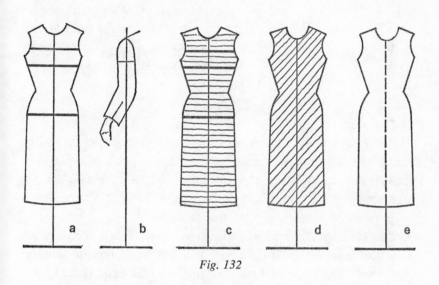

Fig. 132

This is how the grain should appear in your garment:

The center-front and center-back grain hang at right angles to the floor (Fig. 132a). This places the horizontal grain at right angles to the center-front and center-back grain. Properly placed, it is parallel to the floor.

Check the correct position of the horizontal grain across the chest, across the bust, across the shoulder blades, and across the hips—both front and back (Fig. 132a). It may be helpful to mark the horizontal grain with guide-basting also (long floats on the right side)—at least until you train your eye to see it (Fig. 132e).

If the garment is cut on the horizontal grain or on the bias, mark the center front and center back with guide-basting (Fig. 132c and

132d). It is much easier, quicker, and more accurate to use hand guide-basting on bias-cut garments.

Wherever the grain departs from its correct position, unpin or release the seam involved and reset in the proper position.

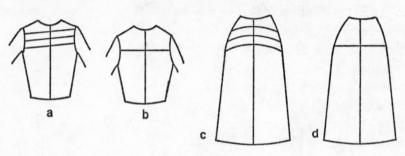

Fig. 133

FOR INSTANCE:

If the crosswise grain slants out of its horizontal position as in Fig. 133a, release the shoulder seams, set the grain aright, and repin (Fig. 133b). If the crosswise grain droops as in Fig. 133c, release the side seams, set the grain aright, and repin (Fig. 133d). This same procedure is followed in each part of the garment.

Let us see how this works in the set-in sleeve. When correctly set, the vertical grain hangs at right angles to the floor from the shoulder to the elbow. The horizontal grain is parallel to the floor (Fig. 132b).

(Do not be concerned with the grain in the lower portion of the sleeve—elbow to wrist—which departs from this position because of the elbow darts or the shape of the sleeve.)

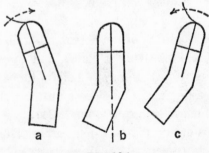

Fig. 134

If the lengthwise grain of the sleeve tilts forward as in Fig. 134a or backward as in Fig. 134c, unpin the sleeve or release the stitching and *dial the cap* to the correct position (Fig. 134b). It really is just as simple as that!

When the entire garment is fitted correctly for grain, it is possible to trace the horizontal grain completely around the bodice front, sleeve, and bodice back in a continuous line which is parallel to the floor. The same can be done for the skirt.

Sometimes *out-of-position* grain *indicates the need for more dart control.* When this is so the drooping grain is accompanied by a deep wrinkle or fold (Fig. 135a) just crying out to be put into a dart (Fig. 135b) or control seam (Fig. 135c). Wrinkles or folds like these are in reality uncontrolled darts.

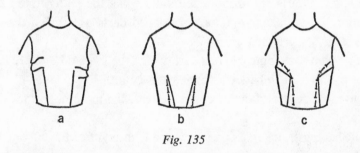

Fig. 135

So you see, the correct grain is more than a question of aesthetics—the weave or design motif in an upright position. It also indicates the proper placement of silhouette seams and the proper amount and placement of dart control. In a very real sense it is the key to good fit.

Fitting for Shape

We have dealt fairly extensively with this subject in Chapter III, The Shape of Fashion.

BRIEFLY, TO REFRESH YOUR MEMORY:

Dart control is the difference between a large measurement and a smaller adjoining one.

The larger the amount of stitched dart control, the greater the resulting bulge in the garment. The smaller the amount of stitched dart control, the less the resulting bulge.

Flat figures, whether heavy or slight, need less dart control because there is less difference between the measurements of adjoining areas.

Shapely figures, whether heavy or slight, need more dart control because there is more difference between the measurements of adjoining areas.

Dart control must be correctly positioned in order to provide the shaping where you need it.

Curved darts or control seams shape more closely to the body than straight darts or seams which provide more ease.

All changes in dart control are made from the high point of the area under consideration.

Designer's darts are unshortened darts while the *pattern* is in construction. Dressmaker's darts are shortened darts used when the *garment* is in construction.

Too much dart control in one dart throws the grain off and produces a sharp bulge. It is better to divide the control.

The more control darts or control seams, the more opportunity for fitting.

All shaping seams must pass over the high point of the curve being fitted or within 1 inch either side of it unless there is auxiliary shaping by other seams, darts, or fullness.

Bulges at the dart point mean that the dart is too large.

Wrinkles (excess or drooping fabric, folds) may mean that more dart control is needed.

"Hiking Up" or *"Poking Out"* may mean that more dart control is necessary in addition to or instead of additional length.

Fitting may reveal the need for more dart control, less dart control, no dart control, or dart control in different places.

Common Fitting Problems in Which Dart Control Is a Factor

BULGES OR POUFS AT DART POINTS MEAN TOO MUCH DART CONTROL (Fig. 136a)

Eliminate some of it (Fig. 136b), or all of it, and shape the garment at the side seams (Fig. 136c). Divide the control or make multiple darts (Fig. 136d). For most people several darts with their more subtle shaping are more flattering than a single bulging dart.

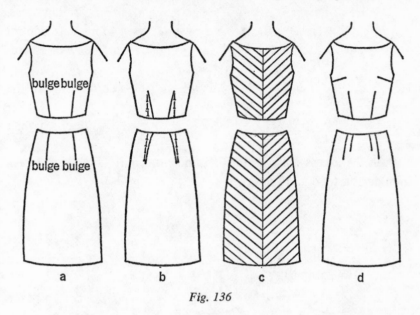

Fig. 136

WRINKLES OR FOLDS DUE TO INSUFFICIENT DART CONTROL

Push the excess material into the nearest seam or dart. Where there is no dart (or seam) create one.

At the Upper Armhole (Fig. 137a)

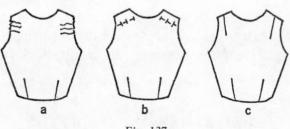

Fig. 137

Push the excess material into the shoulder seam (Fig. 137b) or create a shoulder dart (Fig. 137c).

At the Lower Armhole (Fig. 138a)

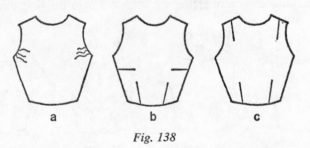

Fig. 138

Push the excess material into an underarm dart (Fig. 138b) or a shoulder dart (Fig. 138c).

At the Side Seam (Fig. 139a)

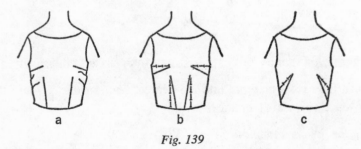

Fig. 139

Push the excess material into the underarm dart and/or the waistline dart (Fig. 139b) or create a new French dart containing all of the control (Fig. 139c). The latter must be consistent with the design.

At the Waistline of Bodice or Skirt (Fig. 140a)

Push the excess material into the waistline darts (Fig. 140b) or create new darts (Fig. 140c). Take some dart control off the side seams.

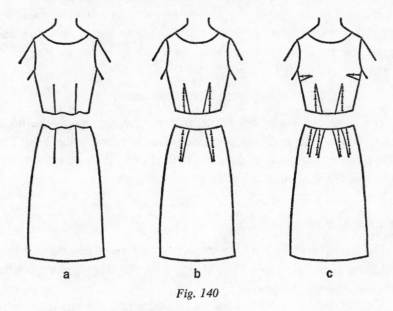

Fig. 140

At the Hem of a Skirt (Fig. 141a)

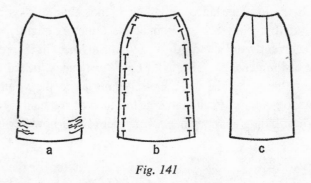

Fig. 141

Release the side seams. Fit the skirt at the hips setting the grain in the right position. Refit and repin the side seams from hips to waist (Fig. 141b). Push the excess fabric into existing darts or create new ones (Fig. 141c). Let the fabric fall naturally at the side seams. Repin.

Whenever a change is made in a dart—either to make it smaller or larger—the seam from which it originates is altered in length. Compensate for this by adding or subtracting as much as is necessary to make it match the seam it must join. If the shape of a section has been altered in any way, retrace it or reconstruct it from the original pattern. *All corresponding seams must be made to match in length and shape. Each pair of dart legs must be made to match in length.*

Fitting the Silhouette Seams

The silhouette seams are seams that outline the figure—the neck, the shoulders, the armholes, the side seams, the waist, the hem. Despite fashion changes in silhouettes, the outlining seams do not depart too radically from the following standards.

THE NECKLINE SEAM

The neckline seam is a very important feature of any design since it is always in view whether one is sitting or standing. It is imperative that the neckline fit just so.

A neckline is as high or as low as fashion would have it, your figure can take it, and you can bare it. In the basic-fitting dress, the neckline is placed at the base of the neck about where a single strand of pearls is worn. In pattern parlance, anything higher than this is a raised neckline, anything lower is a dropped neckline. A slightly dropped neckline (currently the standard for a "natural" neckline) creates the illusion of a slimmer neck. The "poor boy," turtleneck, raised neckline can be as flattering to the not-quite-so-young as to the young. After all, those "dog-collars" fashionable at the turn of the century had the great merit of hiding a crepey neck. However low or however high, the

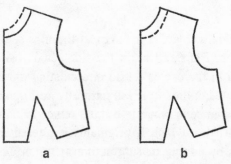

a   b

Fig. 142

neckline must lie smoothly against the body, with no straining or gapping.

It is simplest to make neckline changes in the pattern. If the neckline is too high for you, drop it (Fig. 142a). If it is too low, build it up (Fig. 142b). The broken lines in Fig. 142 show the original neckline, the solid lines the new neckline.

It is practically impossible to raise a neckline once it's been cut. The only way you can build up a too-low neckline is to fill it in as decoratively as possible.

It is easy enough to cut down a too-high neckline. However, be mindful of the fact that dropping a neckline after the garment has been cut will alter the fit. In the dropping, the line of the neck is lengthened and lengthened necklines, as you well know, have a tendency to gap.

Why Dropped Necklines Gap: The block from which a style pattern is made has a straight, vertical line for its center front (Fig. 143a). Your body, however, does not. In profile, your body silhouette is more like Fig. 143b. When you put the two together, you find that the vertical center-front line stands away from the body (Fig. 143c).

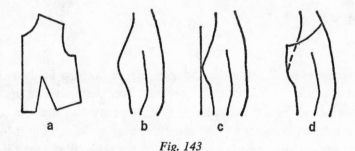

a   b   c   d

Fig. 143

The lower portion of the bodice below the bust is controlled by the darts bringing it into line with the body contour (Fig. 143d). Without the dart control, the upper part of the bodice front remains the straight line. The discrepancy between the center-front line of the pattern and the body contour appears as ease. In a high-necked bodice this is desirable. In a low-necked bodice, the ease produces the gapping (Fig. 143d). To correct the gapping, the length of the neckline must be made to correspond to the body measurement without ease.

How to Correct a Dropped Neckline that Gaps in Front and/or Stands Away from the Neck in Back (Fig. 144a)

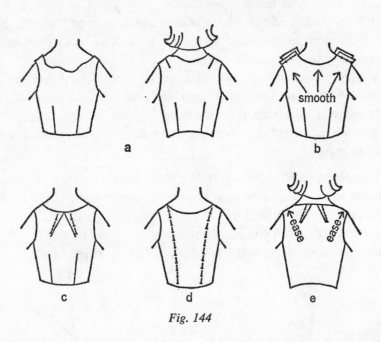

Fig. 144

Front neckline: Release the shoulder seams. Starting at the center front and center back smooth the material over the body and up into the shoulder seam. Repin. In doing this, you may find that the front and back shoulder seams no longer match at the neckline (Fig. 144b). Correct the neckline by trimming some of the seam allowance off the back neckline and using as much of the front seam allowance as possible to make a continuous line from center front to center back. A similar adjustment must be made at the armhole where front and back armhole seams no longer meet.

Other Solutions: If consistent with the design, create neckline darts (Fig. 144c). If there is a control seam, push the excess fabric into it (Fig. 144d).

Back neckline: A back neckline that stands away from the body can be corrected by creating a neckline dart (Fig. 144e). So there will not be too many darts in one small area, stitch the back neckline dart as a dart dart but ease the amount of the original shoulder dart into the front shoulder.

THE SHOULDER SEAM

The shoulder seam lies along the crest of the shoulder just *slightly* forward of the trapezius muscle from the base of the neck to the shoulder socket (Fig. 145a). CAUTION—don't bring this so far forward that it looks like a yoke.

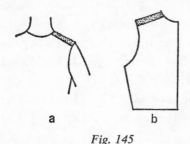

a   b

Fig. 145

This forward position of the shoulder seam creates a slightly longer back neckline and hangs the garment from the shoulder.

When the back neckline is too short, the garment keeps sliding to the back. The correction for this is to add to the back shoulder thereby lengthening the back neckline and the back armhole (Fig. 145b).

The shoulder seam is perhaps the most difficult seam to position correctly. It requires a sensitivity to placement and a good eye. It must be just right—not too far forward, not too far backward.

To avoid the problem and provide an uncomplicated fit, many designs eliminate the shoulder seam by extending the back over the shoulder to the front in a yoke (Fig. 146a) or vice versa. Fitting done on the yoke seam does not require quite the precision that the shoulder seam does.

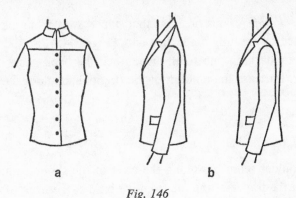

a   b

Fig. 146

Sometimes instead of the classic straight-across shoulder seam, the shoulder line is designed as a slanting seam—back to front or front to back (Fig. 146b). (The slanting shoulder seam is characteristic of many men's suits.) If you must normally make pattern changes in the shoulder area to accommodate your figure, be sure to make corresponding changes in these designs or any similar ones. Next time you study your pattern book observe how many other design devices there are for circumventing the problem of shoulder-seam placement.

THE ARMHOLE SEAM

The armhole seam in a dress with a set-in sleeve starts from any point on the shoulder either currently fashionable or particularly becoming. Generally, the top of the sleeve joins the shoulder seam at the outside of the prominent shoulder bone (socket). It curves over the top of the shoulder, continues in a slightly curved line—deeper in front, shallower in back—to the crease where arm and body join. (Remember there is some ease here.) Below this, the seam swings into the underarm curve—deeper in front, shallower in back—to a depth of ½ to 1½ inches below the armpit (Fig. 147).

The exact position of the back armhole is best determined when the arms are brought *moderately* forward. This provides enough room for the forward movement of the arms.

Many designers feel that more sleeve action is achieved by a high and close-fitting armhole. They point out that the lower the underarm drop, the more the bodice is lifted when the arms are raised.

Any fitting faults that extend to the armhole become much more obvious when the sleeves are set in. Fit the bodice carefully before setting the sleeve on the armhole ease.

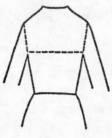

Fig. 147

Shoulder-pad Allowance: When the design calls for shoulder pads, an allowance for them has been made in the pattern. All fitting should be done with them in place. Should you wish to use shoulder pads when they are not called for, allowances for them must then be made on the shoulder and armhole seams of the pattern. Directions follow.

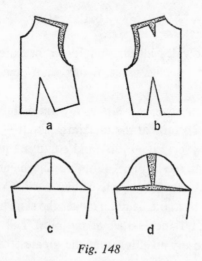

Fig. 148

1. Raise and extend the shoulder seam half the thickness of the pad, both front and back (Figs. 148a and b). If the shoulder pad is

½ inch thick, let us say, then raise and extend the shoulder seam ¼ inch in front and ¼ inch in back. The new shoulder line tapers to the neckline; the new armhole meets the original armhole at the point where it swings into the underarm curve (Figs. 148a and b).

A corresponding adjustment needs to be made on the sleeve cap.

1. Draw a slash line across the cap from underarm to underarm (Fig. 148c).

2. Draw a slash line at right angles to this line extending to the top of the cap (Fig. 148c).

3. Slash on these lines.

4. Raise the cap to the amount of the thickness of the pad as illustrated (Fig. 148d). This spreads the top of the cap in just the right amount for the raised and extended shoulder (Fig. 148d).

5. Locate a new shoulder marking at the center of the spread.

If you wish to dispense with shoulder pads in a design that calls for them, reverse the entire procedure for adding the shoulder-pad allowance.

THE SIDE SEAM

The side seam divides all circumference measurements into front and back. The correct placement of this seam creates a balance between them.

In profile, the side seam appears as a continuation of the shoulder seam (Fig. 149a). It starts at the underarm about ½ inch back of the middle of the armscye (Fig. 149b) and continues in a plumb line to the floor. As you can see in Fig. 149b, this placement of the side seam creates a deeper front armhole curve than back. Continuing straight down from underarm to the hemline makes the skirt front 1 inch larger at the waistline and 1 inch larger at the hips. This latter may come as a surprise to those who think that the greatest bulk is at the seat of the skirt.

When the arms hang naturally at the side, the middle fingers should touch the side seams of the skirt.

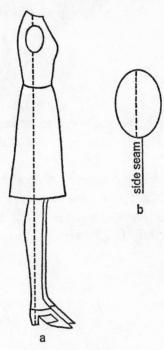

Fig. 149

If the side seam swings forward (Fig. 150a) or backward (Fig. 150b), release the seam. Repin the skirt at the hips making sure that the grain line is in the right position. The skirt is really balanced at the hips. Check the dart control front and back. Pin-fit the side seams from hips to waist. Allow the fabric to hang naturally from the hips.

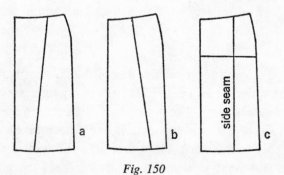

Fig. 150

Pin-fit the side seams adding to or subtracting from front or back as necessary (Fig. 150c), to bring the seam into the correct position.

THE NATURAL WAISTLINE

The natural waistline is located where the circumference of the body is smallest. In motion, the waistline appears higher than when one is standing still. For this reason, fit it slightly lower than it is in reality (Fig. 151a).

If you are short and heavy-bosomed, you will undoubtedly want to make the waistline even lower than this for a longer, slimmer line (Fig. 151b). Very tall or long-waisted figures look better when the waistline is raised slightly (Fig. 151c).

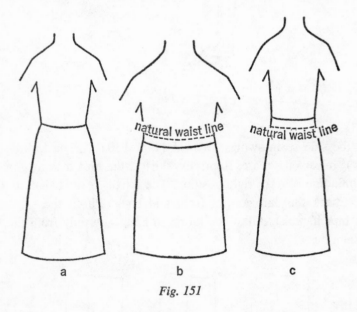

Fig. 151

Patterns are constructed on the theory that a "normal" waistline is tipped slightly forward (Fig. 152a). In many figures (swayback), just the opposite is true. The waistline tips backward (Fig. 152b).

The position of the waistline seam is easily determined. Pin a tape measure snugly at the waist. Place it so that the bottom of the tape rests in the hollow of your natural waistline or in the position you

Fig. 152

would like for a waistline. Place a row of pins on the garment along the bottom of the tape measure. The width of the tape measure provides the necessary length ease. So that you won't lose the marking, run a line of basting to replace the pins as soon as the skirt or bodice is removed from the figure. This line of basting becomes the stitching line for the waistline. Mark bodice and skirt in the same way and join at the markings.

A waistband joins the skirt along this line, too.

When the waistline is properly set, there is no wrinkling, pulling, or straining.

THE HEMLINE

There's no use fighting it! You'll save yourself a lot of inching-up and inching-down if you set your hem at a fashionable length to begin with. This does not mean that you have to wear a miniskirt if you're not the type just because it is fashionable. Hems are not only a matter of how-far-from-the-floor. They are part of a total look. If that particular total look is not for you, neither is the length of the skirt.

Some women live their fashion lives in the constant fear of imminent change of skirt lengths. When drastic changes in skirt lengths do occur, they are usually accompanied by drastic changes in silhouette, too. It is not only that we are caught with our hems down—or up— when a fashion change occurs; the total look is wrong. We have to go to work on new wardrobes anyway.

Optical illusions cause skirts of the same length to appear longer or shorter than they really are. Because a narrow skirt rides up when in motion it seems shorter than a full skirt that measures the same distance from the floor. Because a full skirt hangs away from the body it is not affected by movement, therefore it looks and actually is longer. This means that your straight skirt should be a trifle longer than you would normally set it while your full skirt can afford to be a little shorter.

To mark a hemline you need a skirt marker and a good friend. Despite all the tricks and all the self-marking gadgets, the most accurate hemline is one marked for you by someone else.

Try on the garment wearing the foundation garments and the shoes and stockings you plan to wear with the outfit. That you need the foundation garment is obvious. Perhaps not so obvious is the fact that your posture in a particular heel height affects the length. So, too, does the style, color, and texture of shoes and stockings. Remember that it's the continuity of the complete outfit that determines the length. Stand still and let your sewing buddy move around you. A change in position may throw off the accuracy of the hemline.

THE LENGTH OF THE SLEEVE

A short sleeve is as short as the season, the fashion, and the beauty of your arms permit. A long sleeve ends at or just below the wristbone in a dress. In a coat, just above the first thumb joint. (They do say this is where the expression "rule of thumb" originated.) There are many lengths in between the short-shorts and the long-longs. These are dictated by the design of the garment largely. As with other elements of design, you may take some liberties with sleeve lengths.

All circumference seam lines are curved to follow the natural curves of the body. No matter how straight the line appears when worn, in the pattern and in the garment the neckline, the bustline, the waist-line, the hipline, the hemline are all slightly curved.

Season to Taste

Recipes give the exact measurements. Why, then, the inexact "Season to taste"? Because, following the rules isn't always enough to produce just *the* right degree of deliciousness. One must use one's judgment, too.

So it is in fitting. If you follow all the preceding rules will your garment fit flatteringly? Hopefully, yes. Possibly not. Here is where that "season to taste" comes in. Use your knowledge of optical illusions and your artist-eye to point up your good features and hide your not-so-good ones.

Would your garment look better IF

the shoulder seams were a little wider? or narrower?
the shoulder seams were moved forward? or backward?
there were a little more ease across the chest? across the back?
  across the bust? there were a little less ease?
the waistline or hipline were not quite so snug or so loose?
the waistline were raised? or lowered?
the side seams were moved forward? or backward?
the garment had more shaping? or less shaping?
the sleeves were wider? or narrower?

Sometimes adhering to the rules may be downright wrong for you. Take a round-shouldered person who strictly follows the rule for the placement of the shoulder seam only to find the slightly forward position of the seam emphasizes her round-shoulderedness. She would be wise to ignore the rule and keep the shoulder seam somewhat toward the back. Or, take the woman with the heavy posterior who follows the rule for the plumb-line placement of the side seam and ends up emphasizing a part of her anatomy it would be wisdom to minimize (Fig. 153a).

The solution for the latter is to ignore the rule for the placement of the side seam. Instead she should make the skirt front wider at the

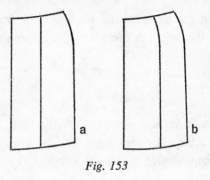

Fig. 153

hips as well as at the waistline in a pleasing proportion, gently curve the side seam from waistline to hips, then continue straight to the floor (Fig. 153b). If she does this the space from center front to center back will be divided in such a manner that the back appears smaller.

See what tricks of magic lines and spaces can perform?

Fit or Fake

In addition to all of the above you must also know when to fit and when to fake. Remember that you are trying to create an illusion of symmetry in a body balance distinguished by its asymmetry.

Fit out those deviations from the standard where they won't show or attract attention or distort the balanced look of the garment.

Fake a balanced look where it will show no matter what you must do to get it.

FOR EXAMPLE:

You may fit each shoulder differently for slope but you must make your shoulders equal in width even if they are not. Since no one sits or stands at rigid attention for any length of time, who can tell which shoulder is up and which down? However, were you to make one shoulder narrow and one wide you would end up looking lopsided like a late-period Picasso.

Make your armholes and sleeves the same size though one may fit a higher shoulder than the other. Who will ever realize they are not the same?

Make your darts the same height and equally distant from the center but you may have a different amount of control in each. No one will ever know how much is stitched into the darts. They're on the underside where they will never show. However, everyone can see the height and placement of the darts because there they are—right out where they can be seen.

For beautiful fit, you must learn to create the illusion of symmetry where it doesn't exist and the illusion of perfection for a figure of imperfections.

Is It Worth It?

Theoretically, it should be possible to make most styles fit most figures. Whether it is worth all the time and trouble to do so is a very real question.

For many styles and many figures so much needs doing that one must practically redraft the pattern. This is an impossibility for the average sewer. Even if she did all that was necessary to make it fit there is still the question as to whether the reshaped, compromised result has the appeal of the original design.

If, after a reasonable try, the style you are working with does not lend itself fairly readily to adjustment, better forget it. Get a different pattern or buy another dress—that is, unless you are the terribly determined type who will admit no failure.

Chapter VI

FITTING AIDS

HOW TO MAKE AND USE A BASIC PATTERN AND A DRESS FORM

A Basic Pattern, a Dress Form, and You! No, this is not the title of a song. It is a formula for fitting that can assure you flattering clothes.

Unless you particularly enjoy going through the lengthy business of measuring and altering every pattern you plan to use, there is no need to—if you have a basic pattern. Unless you have some sew-mate who will come a-running every time you need a fitting, you would do well to provide yourself with a dress form.

A *basic pattern* is a paper portrait of you. It is made to your measurements and fitted to your figure. It has built into it all the many little departures from the standard that say "You." It is both a cutting guide and a fitting guide. It saves hours of guesswork and complicated arithmetic. It avoids costly mistakes in cutting that cannot be corrected later on.

A *dress form* is a kind of sculptured portrait of you. Sans head, sans arms, sans legs it is not the familiar You. For fitting purposes, that's fine for it makes you capable of evaluating what's left more objectively.

As with many portraits, you may not be pleased with what you see. However, these portraits are the You that needs fitting. As such, they are invaluable aids.

What You Need to Make the Basic Pattern

Most of the following are already in your sewing equipment. A number of the drafting tools have been referred to previously in Chapter IV. So that you may get them all together for the making of your basic pattern, a list follows.

1. A roll of wide shelf paper, wrapping paper, or firm tissue paper. Old pattern issues are excellent for patches and insertions. (This is a good chance to use up some of those old patterns you've been hoarding for years, hoping someday to make them up.)

2. A pencil of medium-soft lead and a red pencil for corrections. These should have well-sharpened points.

3. A 12-inch ruler and a yardstick.

4. A curved ruler, sometimes called a "curved stick" for the hipline curve.

5. A Dietzgen No. 17 transparent curve (armscye). A Dietzgen No. 16 transparent curve for subtler curves.

6. A 45° triangle (used for establishing right angles) or a tailor's square.

7. A tracing wheel and dressmaker's carbon paper.

8. Two pairs of scissors—one for cloth, the other for paper.

9. Scotch tape.

10. Pins.

11. Heavy string, enough to go around your waist and hips.

12. Tape measure.

13. Unbleached muslin or inexpensive cotton material for testing the pattern.

14. Manila tag or heavy paper for the final and permanent basic pattern.

15. A standard size basic pattern. Each of the pattern companies has one. You may find them listed in the catalogues by different names —foundation pattern, master pattern, try-on pattern, shell pattern, basic fitting shell, etc.

If you tend to choose the designs of one particular pattern company over the others, choose that company's basic pattern. It will correspond to the basic block from which their style patterns are created.

If no basic pattern is available to you, a satisfactory one can be pieced together from any patterns in your collection that contain the following features.

These five pieces (and only these) *make up the basic pattern* (Fig. 154).

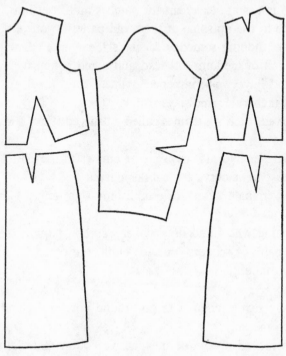

Fig. 154

The *bodice front* should have a high, round (jewel) neckline that fits the base of the neck and an armhole for a set-in sleeve. Most commercial basic patterns have divided dart control. While the pattern fits better this way, it often complicates pattern comparisons and pattern changes. It would be preferable to store the dart control in one waistline dart as in Fig. 154. See Chapter III for directions for shifting darts.

The *bodice back* should have a high, round neckline fitting the base of the neck, an armhole for a set-in sleeve, a shoulder dart, and a waistline dart.

The shoulders and side seams of back and front bodices should match.

The set-in sleeve should be long, fitted, and have one dart at the elbow. It must fit the armhole of the bodice plus 1 to 1½ inches ease.

The *skirt front* should have one dart. Its placement on the skirt should match the position of the waistline dart on the bodice though obviously it will not be the same size. The skirt waistline must match the bodice waistline.

The *skirt back* should have one dart that matches the bodice dart in placement. The amount of the skirt dart is different from the amount of the bodice dart. The skirt waistline must match the bodice waistline.

The side seams of the skirt must match.

Some commercial basic-fitting patterns contain additional pieces that are style variations of the basic pattern. These are not necessary for your basic pattern.

The five pattern sections described above contain certain valuable and essential information as to:

Size—the length, width, and proportions that correspond to body measurements at comparable points.

Ease—the amounts added to the body measurements in length and width to allow for movement and comfort.

Dart control—the standard amount and placement for a given size.

Contour—the outline or silhouette of each piece which follows the contour of the body.

With this information as a base, each of the above items are adjusted to personal requirements.

Get the commercial basic pattern in a size that comes closest to your measurements. With the help of a friend, take a complete set of body measurements (see Chapter I).

Prepare the Pattern Pieces

Assemble all the equipment you will need to adjust the pattern. Give yourself plenty of room in which to work. Lay out the five pattern sections of the basic pattern. You're off!

FIRST CUT OFF ALL THE SEAM ALLOWANCES OF THE PATTERN

Seam allowances will only confuse your measuring. Besides we don't need them. Fitting is done on the seam line; this is the only line that interests us. In fact, a final basic pattern is made without seam allowances. This is because seam allowances vary with the fabric used and where the seam happens to be in the garment. In general, the sheerer the fabric, the less the seam allowance; the heavier the fabric, the more the seam allowance. Seam allowances that get trimmed back to practically nothing don't have to be very wide to begin with. So— off with the seam allowances! If the patterns are badly wrinkled, *press* them flat with a warm iron.

Elongate the grain line throughout the entire pattern. This is necessary so that the trial muslin is *cut on-grain*.

MEASURE—COMPARE

Now *measure* your pattern pieces for each item listed in the measurement chart. Remember that the standard commercial pattern already has the ease added to it. You do not need to add any more. Your body measurements need ease added to them for comparison. The standard pattern is only half a pattern. You will need to halve all *your* width measurements. *Compare* your measurements plus ease with the basic pattern measurements at corresponding places.

A LITTLE ARITHMETIC

A little arithmetic will decide where and how much the pattern needs changing. Note the amounts right on the pattern. Don't bother with very small changes—¼ inch or less. These tiny adjustments can be made at the seams in the muslin fitting.

A LITTLE COURAGE

Feel free to cut sections of your pattern apart and adjust for length, width, and dart control (see Chapter IV). Where you slash-and-spread, insert paper in the opening and Scotch tape to position.

A LITTLE JUDGMENT

Make changes only where needed. Though changed for measurements, preserve the classic shape of the neckline and armhole. Use your No. 17 curve to correct these lines or superimpose the original pattern and trace for correct shape.

Make the Pattern Fit Your Measurements

Reread Chapter IV for complete directions on pattern alterations. Adjust your basic pattern accordingly. Come as close as you can to your measurements but don't get overanxious. A seemingly insoluble mathematical problem may literally "take shape" in cloth. When you have gone as far as you can go with your arithmetic, make your trial muslin.

The Trial Muslin

Pattern changes based on measurements alone, no matter how extensive or how accurate, cannot guarantee the proper fit of a garment. It is necessary to test the pattern in actual cloth to take care of posture and curves as well as lengths and widths and proportions.

A shoulder measurement of 5 inches tells you only that the shoulder measures 5 inches. *But* it does not tell you whether that 5 inch shoulder is sloping, square, or scooped (Fig. 155). Cloth alone can define its character.

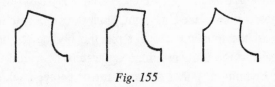

Fig. 155

A trial fitting in fabric may also show the advisability of departing somewhat from the rules of fitting to create an illusion of a more perfectly proportioned figure (see Fit or Fake, page 152).

The test pattern is generally made of unbleached muslin of medium weight. An inexpensive cotton used for the trial run could serve a double purpose: as a test dress and as a housedress when completed. Old sheeting can be used, if it is not too tough for pin-fitting. Whatever you make it of, treat the material as you would the finest satin or brocade. Care in preparation and cutting will help determine the fit.

LET'S GET STARTED!

Straighten the grain of the fabric by tearing both cut ends. Most cotton fabrics tear easily on the horizontal grain.

Pin the torn edges together. Pin the selvages together. If the material does not lie perfectly smoothly, dampen it and press it to position.

Lay out the corrected pattern on the cloth making sure that the grain line is parallel to the selvages throughout the entire pattern.

Cut out the cloth leaving 1-inch seam allowances on all edges but the neck. Make this seam allowance ½ inch.

Trace all the seam lines and darts on the muslin with the dressmaker's carbon paper and a tracing wheel.

Mark the center front and center back very clearly with colored pencil. It is often helpful to mark the horizontal grain across the chest, across the back, and across the hips, both front and back.

Clip all curved edges—at the neck, the armholes, the sleeve, the underarms.

Pin all darts and seams very closely and very carefully *along* the stitching lines. (Pins placed at right angles to the stitching line restrict the fit of the muslin.) Do not pin the bodice to the skirt, yet. Fitting is easier if the units are done separately first, and then joined.

Leave an opening at either center front or center back so that you can get in and out of your muslin.

Try on the muslin with all the markings and pins to the outside (right side). If they are on the inside (wrong side), your muslin may look more like a finished dress but your fitter will not be able to get at the pins for the fitting.

FIT YOUR MUSLIN

Reread Chapter V on Fitting. Keep it handy for reference. Your "Sewing Buddy" and a full-length mirror are necessary for this next operation—the fitting. That you cannot do this without your best sewing friend goes without saying. The mirror is a must for both of you. It is often easier to judge a fitting in a mirror. (I have not yet figured out why this should be so but it is.)

For each of the pattern sections—bodice, skirt, sleeve—the following points must be considered:

1. Size and ease
2. Grain
3. Dart control
4. Silhouette seams
5. What looks best on you

Suggested Sequence for Fitting

BODICE

1. With the vertical grain in the correct position, pin the center front and back to your slip at the waist. This will hold the bodice at fixed points.

2. Clip the neckline as far as necessary to bring the muslin into position at the base of the neck.

3. Check the horizontal grain across the chest, across the back, across the bust.

4. Fit the shoulders.

5. Fit the bust.

6. Fit the back both at the shoulders and at the waistline.

7. Fit the side seams.

Often, shoulders, bust, back, and side seams are pinned tentatively until the fitting is worked out.

8. Establish the neckline. Draw a line around the base of the neck from center front to center back. Duplicate the curve on the other side.

9. Establish the curve of the armhole. Start at the correct position on the shoulder. Draw a line from the shoulder point down the front armhole to the underarm curve. Bring the arms moderately forward. Draw the line of the back armhole. Do one armhole and duplicate it for the other.

10. Establish the waistline. Draw a line along the bottom of a tape measure or heavy string pushed into the indention of the waist. Do the entire waistline; right and left sides may need different fitting.

11. Remove the muslin.

12. Mark all the changes made in the fitting on the underside (wrong side) of the muslin. This will assure that the right and left side of the fitting will remain so when stitched.

Correct any "jumpiness" of pin markings.

13. See that all corresponding seams match in length. Ditto for each pair of dart legs.

14. True up all lines with your drafting instruments.

15. Machine baste the muslin on the wrong side.

16. Try on the muslin again to check the fit. Make any necessary refinements. With the bodice muslin on, fit the skirt.

SKIRT

1. With the vertical grain in correct position, pin the center front and back to the bodice at the waist.

2. Pin the hips at the side seams, checking the horizontal grain both front and back.

3. Fit the area between the hips and the waist at the side seams. Fit the front darts and the back darts. The skirt side seam should be a continuation of the bodice side seam. The skirt darts match the bodice darts in placement though not in amount.

4. Continue pinning the side seams from hips to hem.

5. Establish the waistline. See directions for bodice waistline above.

6. Set the hemline. On your pattern, record the number of inches from the floor and the heel height of your shoes.

Repeat Steps 11 to 16 of Bodice Sequence for the skirt. When satisfied with the fit, join the bodice and skirt with machine basting.

SLEEVE

1. Pin or baste the sleeve seam from the underarm to a point slightly above the elbow.

2. Gather and block the sleeve cap (see blocking and setting of sleeve, page 218).

3. Pin the sleeve into the armhole.

4. Try on the muslin. Check the position of the grain, the position on the shoulder, the smoothness of the fit across the cap, the line at the front armhole, the line at the back armhole, ease of movement.

5. Refine the fit of the sleeve. Determine the position of the elbow dart.

6. Remove the muslin. Mark any corrections.

7. Pin in the elbow dart. Close the remainder of the sleeve seam.

8. Try on the muslin once more. Check again the set of the sleeve at the cap, at the underarm. Check the fit at the biceps, at the elbow, at the wrist.

9. Establish the sleeve hemline.

Steps 10 to 14—same as 11 to 15 for Bodice

15. Machine baste the entire sleeve. Set the sleeve in the armhole and machine baste.

16. Try on the muslin dress again. Examine it carefully. Refine the fit. Remove the dress.

LINE UP THE MUSLIN

Mark all corrections clearly with colored pencil. Mark new notches wherever they will prove helpful in reassembling the parts of the pattern. For instance: you may need a new shoulder marking on the sleeve cap if you have made any change from its original position. The repositioning of a silhouette seam or the reallocation of dart control makes the original notches invalid; mark new ones.

Take the *marked muslin* apart. Press each section flat. Study the muslin carefully.

Upon examination you will probably find that the right and left sides of each section (bodice front and back, skirt front and back, and possibly sleeves) are not identical. This may be due to the fact that

1. the right and left sides of your figure *are* very different.

2. even the experienced cannot by eye fit both sides identically assuming they are the same.

You will have to make a judgment as to which of the above two factors has caused the discrepancy in the marking and proceed accordingly.

There Is This to Consider: Commercial patterns come to you in half-a-pattern form, generally. Half a pattern on a fold gives a complete pattern when opened out. Half a pattern placed on a double thickness of fabric yields two identical pieces when cut. Whenever possible, layouts are such that two of anything are cut at the same time. This makes cutting easier, faster, and more accurate. Right and left sides are balanced since they are cut alike.

Your basic pattern is used primarily as a cutting guide. It will simplify your comparison, correction, and cutting considerably if in making your basic pattern you settle for one side.

The one side should be the larger side so that you will always have sufficient material with which to work. Keep a record of the smaller side to use in the fitting.

To balance your basic pattern:

1. Fold the muslin patterns—bodice front and back, skirt front and back—on the center lines. Pin both sides—right and left—together.

2. Note the discrepancies between the two sides and decide which to use. Compromise where necessary.

3. Balance the changes: Draw the curve of half the neckline to be duplicated on the other half. Make both shoulders alike in width, both armholes alike in size and shape. Center the darts; equalize the amount of control. (For instance: If the total amount in two waistline darts equals 5 inches, make each dart 2½ inches.) Determine and draw the side seams, the waistline, and the hem. Make both sleeves match.

4. Make all corresponding seams match in length.

5. Make each pair of dart legs equal in length.

6. Make sure the sleeve cap fits the armhole with the correct amount of ease.

7. True up all lines with the appropriate instruments.

The right and left sides of every figure vary to some extent. *If the difference is slight,* a balanced basic pattern with some adjustment in the fitting should prove sufficient.

If the difference is great then *do* make two patterns—one for the right side and one for the left side. Those who have this problem no doubt expect the additional work entailed in cutting and fitting two very different sides.

REFINE THE FIT

Now for another test. Trace the corrected muslin pattern on a fresh muslin or some inexpensive cotton material. (If the original muslin is not too badly marked up you could use it again.) Stitch up all darts and seams. Put a zipper in the test dress.

Once more try on the basic-fitting dress and test it for comfort, ordinary comfort. Sit in it, stand in it, walk about in it. Turn on the television, pick up the baby, answer the phone, walk up the steps, sit down to lunch. Don't do any vigorous calisthenics. This is not a gym outfit, nor even one for active sportswear. It is a fitted dress for general purposes. There are special styles for special activities.

Refine the fit. Take it in a little if it is loose. Let it out a bit where it feels snug. Change the position of a seam if by moving it the fit will be more flattering. Do whatever you wish to make it more comfortable and more becoming. This could mean a series of small changes to perfect the fit. Keep at it until you do.

When you are satisfied that you have made the dress fit as well as you can at this time, take it apart. Press each section, and trace on heavy Kraft paper, wrapping paper, or Manila tag.

The Finished Basic Pattern

Manila tag is fine for a permanent record; it holds up better than paper though it takes more room to store flat. If your storage space is limited to a drawer, then a paper pattern is best for you; it can be rolled up. You may want a paper pattern in addition to the tag one, anyway. Some comparisons are easier to make by pinning the basic pattern and the style pattern together.

True up the pattern once more if necessary. Use your drafting instruments. Commercial patterns are drafted with these tools. Your comparison will be more accurate if the shape of your pattern bears a reasonable resemblance to the commercial pattern.

Be sure to put the necessary symbols and information on the basic pattern. Label each piece, mark the center, draw a sufficiently long grain line, mark notches for easy joining. Note the fact that this pattern has no seam allowance, no shoulder-pad allowance, and no hem. Record the number of inches from the floor the skirt was measured and the height of the heels you were wearing when it was done. Remind yourself that the darts are unshortened and that ease is included. It might be of interest to note the date of the fitting. If you make a pattern for each member of the family for whom you sew, then of course, you'll need names on the patterns.

The Basic Pattern—Another You

Like it or not, the basic pattern is another you. Like that famous "little shadow" of the children's poem, it goes in and out with you. It curves where you do, it bulges where you do, it slopes where you do. Short of a massive and determined program of diet, exercise, or massage it is likely to stay you.

Study your basic pattern honestly and analytically. Recall or research the changes you made in the standard-size pattern to make it fit you. These are a clue to similar changes that must hereafter be made on the style patterns. Where and how much does your figure differ from the standard? Study how the right side of your figure differs from the left. Decide where it is wise to fit and where to fake.

When you have worked a bit with your basic pattern you will come to know what changes need automatically be made on all your patterns to make them fit. If nothing else, you will have learned a great deal about your figure you never knew before and understand at last why you have had trouble fitting your clothes.

Your basic pattern can also help you to decide what size commercial pattern best fits you. It is worth the time and expense to do a little experimenting in order to determine what size needs least alteration. Many a sewer creates her own fitting problems by using the wrong size.

The Basic Pattern is the Start of a Style

The basic pattern is style reduced to its minimum figure requirements. In the flat-pattern method, all new designs are derived from it. New styles are created by shifting the basic control, by dividing it, by using it in seams or in controlled fullness. The pattern is slashed and spread for additional fullness. Its over-all area is often broken into smaller areas shaped with interesting style lines. Whatever the design innovations, the start of a style is the basic pattern.

Each new pattern with which you work demands interpretation. This is why a knowledge of patternmaking is of such great importance to all sewers even if they never design or create an original pattern.

Instant Patterns

It is possible to compare your five-piece basic pattern with any style that comes along for vital information as to length, width, shape, ease, etc. The comparison is made much easier if you have a set of appropriate patterns made up and ready for instant use. For instance: a style that features a French underarm dart is much easier to compare when you have a ready pattern that also features a French underarm dart. It is much easier to compare a one-piece dress or an overblouse with a ready hip-length basic pattern. For "instant" comparison, a set of "instant" patterns is a great time-saver. Consider making a set that contains those style features you favor.

You will find information on shifting and dividing darts in Chapter III. Basic jacket and coat patterns will be found in Chapter V. Following are directions for making two additional ones—a basic hip-length pattern and a basic pants pattern.

How to Make the Basic Hip-length Dress Pattern

BACK (Fig. 156)

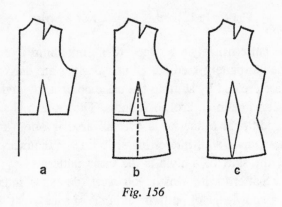

a   b   c

Fig. 156

1. Trace the bodice-back pattern leaving sufficient room on the paper for the rest of the pattern.

2. Extend the center-back line to the back-hip depth (see Personal Measurement Chart, page 71) (Fig. 156a).

3. Lay the skirt pattern on in such a way that the center back is superimposed on the newly drawn line (or parallel to it; see Front —Fig. 157b). The waistlines of the bodice and the skirt touch at the side seams (Fig. 156b).

4. Trace the skirt side seam from waist to hips (Fig. 156b).

5. Draw the hipline from center back to the side seam. This is a slightly curved line (Fig. 156b). The back hipline should be equal to half the back-hip width plus half the back-hip ease. If it measures more than this, the excess can come out as dart. See Front—Fig. 157c.

6. Drop a line from the bodice dart point to the hipline, parallel to the center back (Fig. 156b).

7. Connect the bodice-back dart to the new dart point on the hips (Fig. 156c).

FRONT (Fig. 157)

If the bodice-front basic pattern does not already have an underarm dart, divide the waistline dart control so it does have one. Throw as much dart control into the underarm dart as will bring the side seam into a line that more nearly follows the contour of the body at the underarm seam.

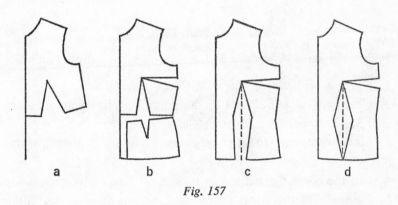

a   b   c   d

Fig. 157

1. Trace the bodice-front basic pattern leaving sufficient room on the paper for the rest of the pattern.

2. Extend the center front line to the front hip depth (see Personal Measurement Chart, page 71) (Fig. 157a).

3. Lay the skirt pattern on in such a way that the center front is parallel to the newly drawn line and the waistlines of bodice and skirt touch at the side seam (Fig. 157b).

4. Trace the skirt side seam from waist to hips (Fig. 157b).

5. Draw the hipline from the center front to the side seam. This is a slightly curved line (Fig. 157b).

6. Drop a line from the bodice dart point to the hipline, parallel to the center front (Fig. 157c).

7. Measure the front hipline of this pattern. Subtract your hip measurement (half the front-hip width plus half the front-hip ease). The difference between the two comes out as dart on the hipline.

8. Center the amount of the hip dart control over the bust-to-hip

dart line (Fig. 157c). If the measurement warrants it, the dart can be brought to a point on the hipline (Fig. 157d).

9. Connect the bodice-front dart to the dart points on the hipline (Fig. 157c and d).

On both front and back hip-length patterns correct the angularity of the side seam at the waistline with a gentle curve. Make the front and back curves match. An easy way to do this is to perfect one pattern, cut it out, then trace the new curve on the other pattern.

The Basic Pants Pattern

Follow the same procedure as for making a basic-dress pattern.

1. Select a very simple shorts or slacks pattern.

2. Check the measurements of the pattern against your measurements. See Personal Measurement Chart, page 76.

3. Make whatever pattern changes are necessary in length, width, shaping.

4. Cut the corrected pattern in muslin or inexpensive cotton.

5. Carefully fit the pants following the same rules as for fitting any other garments with regard to grain, dart control, seam lines, ease, and what looks best for you.

6. When satisfied with the fit, clearly mark all the changes made. Take the pants apart. Press each section flat.

7. Decide what fitting lines to use for your pattern, balancing right and left sides.

8. Correct any "jumpiness" of pin markings. Make all corresponding seams of equal length. Make all dart legs equal. True up all lines with the appropriate instruments.

9. Trace the corrected muslin to heavy paper or Manila tag.

CULOTTES

For those who still feel hesitant about wearing trousers yet like the comfort and freedom of movement that pants permit, there are culottes, currently very fashionable.

Since culottes are a combination of skirt and trousers, they present fitting problems that are characteristic of both. A basic culotte pattern can be made from your skirt basic pattern plus some of the pants measurements.

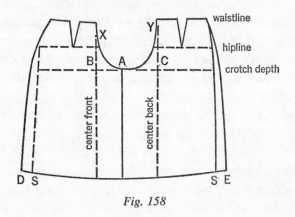

Fig. 158

In Fig. 158 AB equals half the skirt-front measurement at the crotch line less 1 inch.

AC equals half the skirt-back measurements at the crotch line plus 1 inch.

DS and ES are 1 inch added to the side seams to provide walking room, AX and AY are crotch curves which may be traced from the pants pattern.

As with the other basic patterns, it would be well to test this one in cloth. Perfect the fit. Transfer the pattern to paper or tag.

The above patterns plus those covered earlier in the book should give you a set of basic patterns useful for most purposes.

How to Use Your Basic Pattern with a Style Pattern

At last you have your much-wanted basic pattern; in fact, you have several of them. You learned much about fitting in the course of making them and that's all to the good. Now *you must learn to use your basic pattern* to get the most out of it. Just remember that your basic pattern is a guide—not a panacea!

Style vs. Fit

When you select a commercial pattern from the hundreds that are offered to you, you do so because you like its style. The basic pattern is used to make that style fit your figure. Every style pattern was once a basic pattern. If, in an effort to ensure fit, you remove the style features, then you return the style pattern to its original block form. That would defeat the purpose of buying a commercial pattern. Therefore, it becomes very important to learn to distinguish which features of a design are meant primarily for style and which primarily for fit, though admittedly it is hard to make the separation. (See Chapter VIII—How to Choose a Style with an Eye to Its Fitting Potential.)

Your basic pattern deals with minimums. It contains the least amount necessary for length, width, ease, shaping. The designer may have other ideas. (Indeed, we hope he does!) The commercial pattern contains style features that may add length or fullness for effect. Don't change or eliminate the design features in the pattern. If you are uncertain about how a style will look on you or what modifications would make it more flattering, make a test muslin before you make a decision on changes.

Unfortunately, both these cautions are necessary. For some sewers the temptation is very great to reduce the style to that basic pattern one knows fits so well.

A Few Reminders

1. The darts in your basic pattern are unshortened while the darts in the style pattern are shortened. In the final pattern to be used for cutting and construction, the darts will be shortened.

2. Your basic pattern has no seam allowance on it while the style pattern does. Comparison is made from seam line to seam line. A garment fits on the seam line not on the cutting edge.

3. Your basic pattern has no hem; the style pattern does.

4. Your basic pattern has no shoulder-pad allowance. Check the sewing directions to see if your style pattern does. Make adjustments when necessary.

5. Use a colored pencil or pen for marking so that the changes will be clearly visible.

6. The style pattern should be a complete record of all the necessary changes. The same changes will affect the interfacing, the underlining, the lining, and perhaps an interlining. Tuck, pin, patch, Scotch tape, insert paper, write notes to yourself, do anything that is necessary to incorporate the changes right into the pattern. Don't rely on your memory. You may be diverted a dozen times during the course of laying out your pattern and cutting your material.

Simple Pattern Comparisons

BODICE

1. Place the bodice of the tissue style pattern over the basic pattern matching center front or back at the waistline.

2. Compare the two for length and width. Make whatever adjustment is necessary to bring the upper part of the bodice into such position that you can compare the neck, the shoulders, and the armholes. This may mean lengthening or shortening the pattern either above or below the dart.

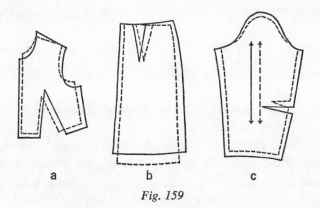

a   b   c

Fig. 159

The broken lines represent the original pattern. The solid lines show the correction from the basic pattern.

3. Trace the entire contour (all outside seam lines) from your basic pattern (Fig. 159a).

4. Check the position, height, and amount of the dart control. Alter accordingly by tracing from your basic pattern (Fig. 159a).

SKIRT

1. Place the skirt style pattern on your basic pattern, matching the center front or back at the waistline.
2. Compare the length and width. Trace the entire contour from the basic pattern (Fig. 159b).
3. Check the position, length, and amount of dart control. Make the necessary changes by tracing from your basic pattern (Fig. 159b).

SLEEVE

1. Place the sleeve style pattern on your sleeve basic pattern matching the grain. One grain line need not necessarily fall directly over the other in which case it must be parallel to it (Fig. 159c). Match the underarms at the side seams.
2. Compare the sleeves for length and width making such adjustments as are needed. Trace the sleeve cap from your basic pattern (Fig. 159c). (Make certain that the armhole of the bodice is just right for it.)
3. Check the position, length, and amount of the elbow dart control.

Make any necessary changes by tracing from your basic pattern.

Comparisons with More Complex Patterns

It is not likely that many of your pattern comparisons will be quite so simple as those described above. However, the general method of comparison is the same. (It might be well to practice a few simple comparisons before you plunge into more complex ones.)

When the bodice, skirt, or sleeve of your style pattern is composed of several sections, first pin together all the sections that complete each unit, then compare the unit with the basic pattern for length, width, contour, and dart control. Do not join the units.

FOR EXAMPLE: Pin together all the sections that complete the bodice front, the bodice back, the skirt front, and the skirt back for the comparison (Fig. 160).

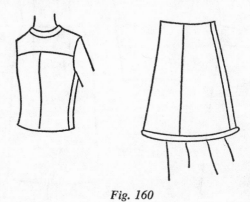

Fig. 160

When the style depends on extra fullness for its effect, fold into position and pin in place all pleats and tucks. Gathers, shirring, drapery can be pinned into tiny folds or pleats. Compare with the basic pattern.

If the pattern pieces are too numerous or too bewildering for comparison with the flat paper pattern, try comparison with a "bulging block" pattern. Trace your basic pattern to heavy paper. Close and fasten the darts with glue, pins, Scotch tape, paper fasteners, or whatever else will hold them together. This produces a firm, bulging form (Fig. 161). As a matter of fact an adequate personalized dress form can be made in this way, particularly if you use a firm cardboard and place it on a stand.

Pin the style pattern together. Slip this "bulging pattern" over your "bulging" form. Compare them in the round (or semi-round). Make the needed changes.

A paper "bulging block" has this advantage: it is possible to pin the tissue pattern to it. This can be enormously helpful in comparing some patterns.

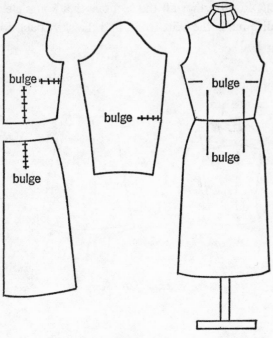

Fig. 161

COMPARING THE BODICE WITH KIMONO SLEEVES

Since the kimono sleeve is all-in-one with the bodice, the comparison is made with the bodice of your basic pattern.

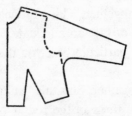

Fig. 162

1. Place the kimono-sleeved pattern over the basic bodice pattern matching the center fronts, starting at the waistline.

2. Make whatever adjustment is necessary to bring the upper part of the bodice into such position that you can compare the necklines and the shoulder lines.

3. Retain the original size and shape of the kimono sleeve for style but trace your shoulder line from the basic pattern for fit (Fig. 162). Correct any angularity that results from the joining.

Sleeves that carry part of the bodice with them—raglan, dolman, strap, etc.—are pinned to the rest of the bodice in the same way yokes are. Make the comparison as directed for the kimono sleeve or for other complex patterns—whichever seems more appropriate to the design.

Make All Corresponding Pattern Pieces Match

When all the pattern adjustments have been made from your basic pattern, be sure to adjust all corresponding pattern pieces that join any you have altered.

Markings and notations should be complete and have a high visibility. It should be possible for you to put the adjusted pattern away today, pick it up a week, a month, a year from now and still understand what you must do.

The Dress Form—Another You

There may be a day when science discovers some cheap, safe, non-toxic, quick-drying, paper-thin, iron-strong, easily applied, easily removed substance that could be sprayed, painted, patted, slapped, molded on the body to make another you. The search for a practical, usable form that duplicates a particular woman's figure has been long, arduous, and to date not completely successful.

The only kind of dress form that is really helpful is one that duplicates your figure. All others are no more help than standard patterns. There are several forms on the market that come close but in fitting, "near-'ems" don't count. Since sewers are handy women they would do better to make their own forms.

The *dressmaker's dummy* is perhaps the most familiar type of personalized dress form. For this one needs a French lining (princess style) of firm muslin, denim, duck, canvas, or any similar fabric cut crosswise of the material for non-stretch.

This lining, fitting skin-tight, is placed over a smaller-size standard dress form and padded to fill out the lining.

The padding may be cotton batting, tissue paper, cotton waste, shredded foam rubber (the kind used for stuffing toys) strips of muslin wound bandage-fashion around the form. The latter can be effectively used in combination with any of the former as a finish. It provides the smooth surface the others lack. A popular dress form currently on the market consists of a molded slab of foam rubber over which the fitted cover is zipped.

The "stuffing" is a secondary matter. What is more important is that the cover be fitted to an *exact replica* of your figure. You'll need help on this.

How to Make the Dressmaker's Dummy

THE FRENCH-LINING COVER

Look at yourself in profile. Note the shape of your silhouette from shoulder to bust, from bust to waist, from waist to hips (Fig. 163).

This is the shaping you find in princess-line garments. They fit so well because they follow so truly the contour of the body. Such shaping is just what we need for our dress form.

1. The first step, then, is to find a pattern for a princess-line dress. It should have the sections illustrated in Fig. 164. It need not have the horizontal seams. Cut off the pattern at mid-thigh length.

2. Alter the pattern to your measurements. Use your basic pattern as a guide.

3. Cut the muslin dress from the corrected pattern. Leave 1½-inch seam allowances for possible adjustments. Mark all seam lines.

4. Pin all seams on the right side, leaving the back open.

5. Slip into the muslin. Have your fitter pin it up the back. Be sure to wear the correct foundation garments and shoes of the heel height you generally favor.

6. Pin the muslin to the foundation garment at center front and back, at the neck, waistline, and hip to hold the cover in place.

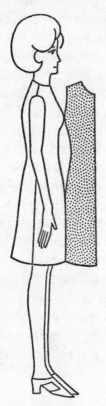

Fig. 163

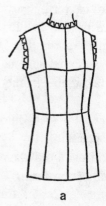

a

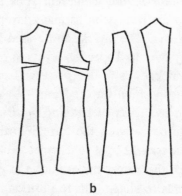

b

Fig. 164

7. *Fit very tight.* The padding has a tendency to stretch the outer fabric.

8. In addition to the lengthwise seams, further define the bust with a horizontal shaping seam across it. (Brassieres frequently have this type of shaping.) Work from the center-front seam to the bust point and from the bust point to the side seam (Fig. 164b). It is possible that the waistline will need some horizontal shaping and seaming, too.

9. Mark the neckline, the shoulder line, the armholes, and the waistline with colored pencil. Be particularly sure that the armhole fits quite tight against the arm. Determine the bottom of the form. Make this 1½ to 2 inches longer than the solid part of the dress form.

10. When satisfied with the fit, remove the muslin cover, transfer the markings to the wrong side, and stitch the seams as marked. Insert a separating zipper at the center back for easy access.

11. Try on the stitched muslin. Make any refinements in fit. You may wish to tighten it further.

12. Trim the seam allowances. Mark the neckline, armholes, and waistline with colored stitching or narrow tape as fitting guides. The shoulder seams, side seams, and center front and back are located by the seaming.

PADDING THE FORM

1. Slip the muslin cover over the form to determine where it needs to be padded. Remove the cover.

2. *Cotton batting* comes in rolls and can be torn apart easily. Build up the form with as many layers as are needed to fill out the muslin cover. The layers can be used horizontally across the form or vertically over it. Taper the layers to produce a curved shaping. Ending all thicknesses at one place will produce a ridge. Pin the cotton batting to position on the form.

If you use *wads of padding or tissue paper,* slip them into place while the cover is on the form. Pin them to position.

3. Cut two 12-by-14-inch pieces of the batting. Fold them to fit and place them over the armholes at each side of the form. Tear off the surplus to shape. Pin to position.

4. Cut two oval pieces of muslin to the size and shape of the arm-

holes plus seam allowance. Stitch these muslin armhole coverings to the muslin cover.

5. Slip the cover over the padded dress form for a trial fitting. Work carefully so that you do not disturb the padding. Zip the cover closed.

6. Examine the form carefully for spots that need extra or less padding. Adjust as necessary by placing small pieces or wads of padding. The muslin should fit very tight over the padded form. The padding should fill out all the curves of the muslin. Remove the cover.

7. Wind strips of bias muslin around the form. This will hold the padding in place and smooth out any lumps or bumps due to the padding.

8. Press the princess-line cover very carefully. Slip it over the completed form and zip it closed. This zippered closing has the advantage of easy removal if future adjustments are necessary. (Figures do change with time.)

A Sleeve Form

It is often useful to have a sleeve form that can be snapped or pinned to the dress form for types of fittings which involve the upper arm or the sleeve. To be helpful, the sleeve form must fit the armhole and the upper arm precisely.

1. Use a two-piece sleeve pattern. The shaping is more natural than a one-piece sleeve (Fig. 165a).

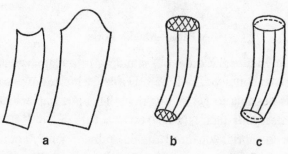

a   b   c

Fig. 165

2. Pin fit very tightly around the arm. Mark the stitching line.

3. Remove the sleeve. Stitch. Press. Stuff.

4. Cut two cardboard retainers—one to fit the armhole, the other to fit the wrist. Adjust the size and shape to fit each precisely.

5. Cut two muslin ovals to the size and shape of the cardboard retainers plus seam allowance.

6. Cover the cardboard with muslin. Turn under the seam allowances and stitch in place.

7. To hold the sleeve stuffing in place before closing each end with the muslin-covered cardboard retainers, make long diagonal stitches across the armhole and wrist openings (Fig. 165b).

8. Turn in the sleeve seam allowances at the armhole and the wrist.

9. Pin the armhole and wrist ovals into position.

10. Pin the sleeve to the armhole of the dress form for testing. The shoulder of the dress form plus the curved cap of the sleeve form should duplicate the lines of your body.

For more roundness: make the oval smaller, bring more fullness over the cap.

For less roundness: remove some of the fullness of the cap.

11. When satisfied with the fit, hand stitch the retainers to the sleeve (Fig. 165c).

12. The sleeve may be attached to the form at the armhole.

BY

1. Sewing loops to the sleeve cap for pinning the sleeve to the form.

OR

2. Sewing snaps to both the sleeve and the form.

A Papier-Mâché Form

If you can endure the ordeal of standing in a clammy, gooey mess for at least two hours you will be rewarded with as truly you a dress form as it is possible to get at this time. This is a papier-mâché form that duplicates your figure (Fig. 166).

To make the form you need a thin, tubular jersey foundation of material to which gummed paper will adhere, a large roll of 1-inch gummed paper tape, several devoted friends and great determination. Better make the form when you are feeling spry on a warm day in a warm place.

Fig. 166

1. Slit the tubular jersey to form armholes.

2. Wearing shoes of the heel height you generally favor and your best-fitting foundation garments, slip the jersey over your body.

3. Shape the jersey to fit your neck and shoulders. See that it fits snugly around the armholes. Lap and tape seam allowances to position. The jersey clings to the form like a bathing suit. If any further adjusting must be done to provide a close fit slash, overlap, and tape the jersey to position.

4. Have one of your helpers prepare the strips of gummed tape. Cut them to length, moisten them with a damp sponge, and keep the fitter supplied. The second helper can apply the tapes as quickly as they are fed to her. Work goes faster if you can persuade a third helper to lend a hand.

5. Strips of moist gummed tape can be worked vertically, horizontally, diagonally, or crosshatched. Use short strips for deep curves; longer strips for more gradual curves.

6. Following is a suggested sequence for applying the tapes.

Foundation Tapes: Cut to needed length, moisten and apply tightly around the waist, the diaphragm under the bust, and the hips. Define the armholes and the neck in similar fashion.

Use short strips to define the bust separation. Work short strips over the bust, shaping and lifting as the work progresses. This is particularly important or the dress form will end up with a squashed and flattened bust line.

Work tapes well over the shoulders.

Overlay Tapes: apply longer strips to the upper back, the bust, the chest, the lower front, the lower back. Often one layer of tape is not sufficiently firm to hold the shape. Reinforce any area that needs it with crosshatching but take great care not to pile up too many layers of tape. While the buildup is necessary, each added layer increases the size of the dress form.

7. When the form is completely taped, cut it open along the center back. Slip out of it very carefully. Using a tape measure pull in the waistline and hipline to actual body measurements. Tape the center back closed.

8. The water, the paper and the glue produce the papier-mâché, which hardens as it dries. To make certain that the form hardens in shape, prop up the bust or any other curve in danger of collapse with wads of tissue paper, cardboard strips, or cardboard cut to shape.

9. When thoroughly dry, apply a coat of shellac both inside and outside.

10. Hang the form over a coat hanger and suspend the two from the ceiling with a strong cord. Or, mount the form on a stand. Get that handy husband or son to make one for you. It is possible you may even be able to buy one.

As with the basic pattern, the dress form can only be valuable to you when you learn how to use it. Keep in mind that the form is about as close as you can get it to your body measurements. Clothing fitted on it must have suitable ease.

Sometimes sewers make the mistake of overfitting when working on the form. This is largely because it is impossible to judge ease in the abstract. Fabric has so much to do with what is the right amount. How comfortable the garment feels and how it moves can best be judged when on the figure rather than on the form. Despite the enormous help that both the basic pattern and the dress form can be, they really do not eliminate the necessity for fitting the garment on the person.

Just You

You're lucky if you have a friend who can help with the fitting. Don't panic if you don't. There is a surprising amount of fitting that you can do for yourself.

You can easily see yourself full-front and profile. If you have a three-way mirror, you can even see your back.

YOU, YOURSELF, CAN

Check the grain, the shaping, the ease, the silhouette seams. See any wrinkles, bulges, gapping, or strain that needs correction. Repin the bust darts, the waistline, and even the side seams considerably above the waist and down to the hips. Mark the shape of a neckline, the roll of a collar, the turn of a lapel, decide where to place buttons, pockets, and trimmings, decide where on the shoulder to set the sleeve.

There are even some back adjustments that can be made without twisting the body too much. For example: you can pinch out and pin an amount that needs to be taken in at the waistline of the back seam. You can reach the back waistline darts.

Places that can't be reached for on-the-spot repinning can certainly be noted as to amounts and positions of changes to be made when the garment is removed. For instance: you may not be able to repin the entire shoulder seam but you can certainly note that it needs to be brought forward or backward by ½ inch. Most people can even reach to place a pin at the place where the seam should be located at the armhole and at the neckline. When these two points are fixed, it is easy enough to pin the correction after the garment is taken off.

It is true that you can't reset your sleeve yourself but you can note that the cap needs to be moved to the front or to the back or that it needs tilting forward or backward.

You may go through a series of judge—note—take off—pin—retry sessions. You have your mirror and your dress form as aides. It is not so much the getting-at-it that is the difficulty with fitting oneself, it's knowing what to do. Only a study of fitting can help you there.

Your ideas of fine fit will change as you grow more experienced, more sensitive to it, and more demanding. You will find yourself constantly refining, polishing, and perfecting. This is as it should be. Any artist, whatever his field, succumbs to this same compulsion. It's a sign you've arrived as a fitter.

Chapter VII

BUILT-IN FIT

HOW TO STITCH IN AND BLOCK IN THE SHAPE
OF FASHION

You could be the best sewer in ten counties and still not know how to fit your clothes but one could hardly be a great fitter without also being an expert sewer. The construction of a garment has everything to do with its fit.

So great is the power of suggestion that a badly made garment appears to fit badly. Any stitching—hand or machine—that puckers, pouches, quilts, wavers, meanders, or otherwise departs from the designated line not only spoils the appearance of the garment, it also spoils its fit. Inadequate pressing not only brands the garment home-made, it actually destroys the shaping. Timidity with trimming scissors not only makes for a lumpy-bumpy look, it really prevents that hard-come-by shaping from functioning. Construction and fit are inseparable.

Clothing construction is a subject so vast and so important of itself that many books are devoted exclusively to it. Since the emphasis of this book is on fitting, we must restrict our discussion of sewing and pressing procedures to those few that best illustrate how directly and how seriously the fit of the garment is affected by its production. An awareness of the interrelation between construction and fit will surely lead the reader to further study.

The Sewer—An Interpreter

The sewer works creatively with what is essentially another's conception. Though she modifies it to suit her purposes and her figure, it is the designer's intent that is paramount. In construction, all techniques stem from this fact. Any that contributes to the realization of the design idea is right to use; any that doesn't is wrong. There are no absolutes. There are only some methods that in a particular garment are more valid than others because by using them one can achieve a desired result easier, faster, and more effectively.

Each dress, each suit, each coat one makes becomes an individual problem to be worked out afresh. This presupposes a knowledge of the many techniques from which to make an appropriate choice.

From the moment a sewer places her first pattern piece on the cloth to the last fond pat, she must so handle her fabric that every motion and every operation will contribute to a three-dimensional form that will encompass her body. In this sense she is sewer-turned-sculptor.

Pattern Placement for Correct Grain

Success in sewing begins with *on-grain cutting of the fabric*. Grain plays such a vital part in fit that the subject has been referred to repeatedly throughout this book (see Index).

BRIEFLY, TO REFRESH YOUR MEMORY

The designer uses the grain to provide the particular kind of look and fit he has in mind.

Every pattern piece no matter how small or how large has the grain marked on it. Make certain that the grain line is sufficiently long to provide on-grain cutting throughout the entire section.

Straighten the grain on both cut ends of the material to restore the cloth to its original rectangular form.

Place the pattern on the fabric in such a way that the straight of goods (grain) is parallel to the selvages the entire length of the garment section. Pin securely.

Cutting Must Be Precise

Cut along the cutting line of your altered pattern. Use long firm strokes of sharp scissors or shears for straight edges. Use short strokes for curves.

Do not use pinking shears for general cutting. They do not give a precise edge. They are meant to be used as an edge finish.

Marking the Fabric

If the garment sections are not joined correctly, obviously the garment will not fit. To assure accurate joining, transfer all pattern symbols to the cloth.

Mark Everything! The more complete the marking, the less work and guesswork when it comes to stitching the pieces of the garment together.

There are three general methods of marking: with tailor's chalk, with dressmaker's carbon paper and tracing wheel, with basting thread. There is much to be said for and against each method. Use whichever is safest and most visible for your fabric.

Stay Stitch Each Cut-out Section

In the much handling between dream and dress, it is very easy to stretch and pull the fabric out of shape. To preserve the grain, the length, and shape of each piece, stay stitch each cut-out section.

Stay Stitching is a line of machine stitching in the seam allowance close to the seam line. Use any thread and eight stitches to the inch.

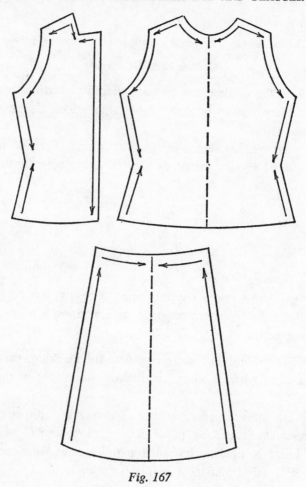

Fig. 167

Stay stitching is *directional* (Fig. 167). There are two rules that apply: stitch from high to low or from wide to narrow. The latter takes precedence over the former. Stay stitch all edges that need to be fixed for either length or shape. Do not stay stitch any edge that will eventually be eased into another or that will not join another.

Never make a continuous line of stay stitching around a corner.

Break the thread at the end of the row and begin again in the new direction (Fig. 168).

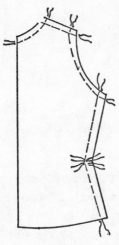

Fig. 168

Precision Machine Stitching Is a Must

A seam is a line of stitching which holds two (sometimes more) pieces of fabric together permanently. To accomplish this, select the correct needle size and thread weight for the fabric you are using. Set the right stitch length and tension.

When the machine is working right, the fabric "rides" smoothly without puckering, creeping, or stretching. The tension is neither too tight nor too loose. The stitches are balanced and lock perfectly on both sides. Everything working correctly produces a seam sufficiently strong to last the life of the garment.

Make each seam and dart the *exact shape and length* it was meant to be. Stitch precisely on the line indicated in the pattern or on the line determined by your fitting. Any deviation from this will alter the planned shape of the completed garment. Take the entire seam allowance. Even tiny fractions of an inch have a way of adding up. Remember that directional stitching preserves the grain. This goes as well for the permanent stitching as for the stay stitching.

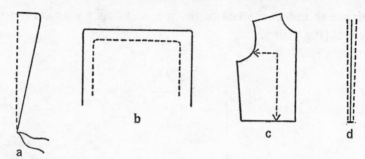

Fig. 169

In *stitching a dart,* start at the wide end and stitch to the dart point tapering off to nothing for a perfect blend (Fig. 169a). Cut the thread and tie the ends in a square knot.

Should you need *to go back over a line of stitching to correct it,* be sure to remove the first stitching. Every added row of stitching stiffens the area. More important, it may affect the contour of the new seam.

Except in very sheer fabrics, it is impossible to get a sharp corner by stitching a 90° angle. In lightweight fabrics, take one stitch across the corner. In heavier-weight fabrics, *take up to three stitches to round a corner slightly* (Fig. 169b).

When a style line comes to a point or a corner, bring the needle down on the point and *stitch away* from it to the end of the seam. Pull the beginning ends of threads through to the wrong side and tie them in a square knot. Bring the needle down into the point once more and stitch in the opposite direction. Pull the beginning ends of the thread through to the wrong side and tie them (Fig. 169c).

In stitching, it is a good rule to *start at the point that requires precision.* If you start at the opposite end, the action of the presser foot on the fabric may push a bubble of excess fabric to the corner or point.

Whenever a slash is to be made in the fabric, the area that contains it needs reinforcement. The reinforcement may be merely machine stitching along the slash line (as for the corners of a gusset insertion) or it may be a facing (as for a placket opening). In any case, *take one stitch across the point* of the slash rather than stitching to the point (Fig. 169d). A blunt point makes it easier to turn back the fabric to the wrong side.

Problem fabrics (bias, knits, chiffons, pile, and other raised fabrics, very sheer or very heavy, very stretchable or very non-easable fabrics) *require special stitching techniques.*

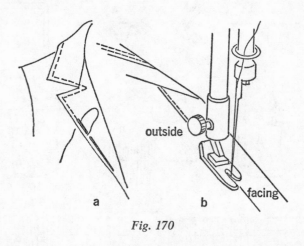

Fig. 170

Topstitching is a line of decorative stitching, either hand or machine, done an even distance in from the finished edge. It is used to hold two layers of fabric in place (Fig. 170a).

Understitching is a line of machine or hand stitching made through facing and the seam allowances of garment and facing. It holds the facing in position on the underside of the garment (Fig. 170b).

Hand Stitching Came Before Machine Stitching

Despite the perfection of the present-day sewing machine, hand stitching is still an important part of clothing construction. The flawless fit of custom-made clothes owes much to the great amount of hand sewing used in their production. Machine stitching is largely flat stitching. Consequently one thinks flat. Fabric-in-the-hand invites shaping. One can better control and actually "feel" the body-conforming curves of the cloth. Wherever flexibility is essential, sewing by hand is the thing to do.

Temporary Hand Stitches

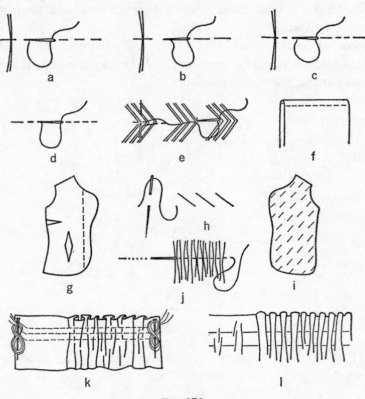

Fig. 171

Just because we live in a machine age does not mean that we have to do everything by machine. In home sewing, there is no doubt that the caliber of both workmanship and fit would many times be greatly improved if more of it were done by hand.

Hand stitching can be temporary or permanent. *Temporary hand stitches* are used *during construction.* They should be so placed and so removed as to avoid damaging the fabric or distorting the shape of the garment. They should be loose, "easy" stitches. Use an appropriate needle, a double thread for marking, a single thread for stitching.

All temporary hand stitches are *variations of the basting stitch.*

Even basting: both stitches and spaces are equal in length on right and wrong sides of the fabric (Fig. 171a).

Uneven basting: a long stitch on the right side of the fabric and a short stitch on the underside (Fig. 171b).

Dressmaker's basting: one long stitch, two short ones (Fig. 171c).

Running stitch: tiny, even stitches woven through the material with an up-and-down wrist motion while the fabric is held still. When the needle is full of stitches, it is drawn through the material (Fig. 171d).

Slip basting (alteration basting): the stitching is done from the right side. It alternates between the fold of fabric and the single layer of cloth. This produces a line of basting on the wrong side useful as a guide for machine stitching; the stitches are invisible from the right side (Fig. 171e).

Edge basting: a line of basting stitches made close to the rolled edge to hold it in place (Fig. 171f).

Guide basting: uneven basting with long floats (thread) on the side that needs the marking (Fig. 171g).

Diagonal basting: diagonal stitch on the upper side, straight stitch on the underside (Fig. 171h).

Tailor basting: diagonal basting with long diagonal stitches on the upper side and short horizontal stitches on the underside (Fig. 171i); used to join two layers of fabric during construction.

Gathering: running stitches drawn up to a predetermined length with the fullness evenly distributed (Fig. 171j).

Shirring: several rows of gathering evenly spaced apart (Fig. 171k).

Gauging: several rows of uneven basting with long and short stitches of each row placed directly under each other; when drawn up, the material falls in deep folds (Fig. 171l).

When *permanent hand stitching* is *the construction,* the stitches should be firm enough to hold. Tacking or finishing stitches should be "easy" stitches never pulled so tight as to restrict the shaping or shorten the length by quilting the fabric.

Backstitch: the hand stitch equivalent of the machine stitch; start one stitch ahead on the right side; working back from left to right, complete the stitch on the surface by inserting the needle where the preceding stitch ended (Fig. 172a). Bring the needle out a stitch ahead and repeat.

Half backstitch: made in the same way as the backstitch with this

Permanent Hand Stitches

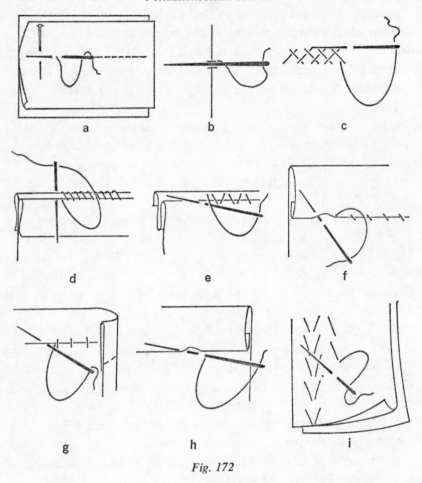

Fig. 172

exception: instead of bringing the needle back to the end of the preceding stitch, bring it over only half (or less) the distance.

Over-and-over stitches: two or more backstitches worked over each
other in place rather than advancing to the left (Fig. 172b).

Catch stitch: a small backstitch worked from lower left to upper
right picking up only one or two threads of the fabric (Fig. 172c).

Overhanding: small stitches worked over and over an edge only deep enough to catch the edges; the stitches are drawn up so that the seam can be opened flat when finished (Fig. 172d).

Slip stitch (blind stitch): an invisible permanent joining worked through an upper and lower fold of fabric; done exactly like the slip basting except that the stitches weave from one fold to the other.

There is a whole family of *hemming stitches* of which the following are most widely used:

Running hemming stitch: a series of small, very loose running stitches weaving back and forth between a garment and the edge of its hem, picking up only a thread or two of the right side of the fabric (Fig. 172e).

Slant hemming: a fast, strong but conspicuous stitch, really a small diagonal basting worked through both hem and fabric; the slanted stitches are visible on both right and wrong sides (Fig. 172f).

Vertical or straight hemming: the stitch used on most hems; can be made practically invisible by tiny stitches catching only one thread of the fabric; stitches on the wrong side are vertical, perpendicular to the hem; stitches on the right side are horizontal, parallel to the hem (Fig. 172g).

Blind hemming: the slip basting worked on the hem (Fig. 172h).

Pad stitching: a small tailor basting used to join permanently an interfacing and an under layer of garment fabric (collars and lapels); stitches are $\frac{1}{4}$ to $\frac{1}{2}$ inch in length in rows that are $\frac{1}{4}$ to $\frac{1}{2}$ inch apart; the needle picks up only a thread of the garment fabric (Fig. 172i).

There are many more permanent hand stitches not included in this listing since they are used more as decorative details and finishes rather than for construction.

Hand Stitched to Shape

Some parts of the garment, cut flat, are worked into figure shapes by hand stitching. Here are two outstanding examples.

THE TAILORED SET-ON COLLAR

In tailoring, the shape of the collar is determined by the direction and tension of the pad stitching worked on the undercollar. (The bias cut makes this molding possible.)

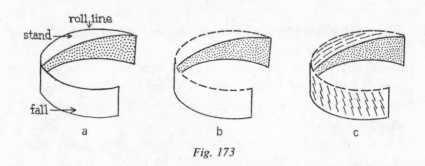

Fig. 173

1. Determine the roll line of the interfacing and mark it. Place the interfacing over the undercollar and pin or baste the two together.

2. Crease the undercollar and its interfacing along the roll line. With interfacing up, curve into a neck shape (Fig. 173a). Hold the collar over the hand in this shape while doing the pad stitching.

3. Using matching thread, make a row of uneven horizontal basting stitches (⅜ to ½ inch) along the roll line (Fig. 173b). The long floats lie on the surface of the interfacing. The needle catches only a thread of the undercollar fabric through the interfacing as in pad stitching. Slightly tug the stitching at the end of the row to create the curve.

4. Pad stitch the stand of the collar with parallel rows of similar uneven horizontal basting. Tug the thread slightly at the end of each row to produce the inside curve of the collar. (Don't overdo this!) The rows are ⅜ to ½ inch apart. Make as many rows as will fill the stand to the seam line. Note that the direction and tension of this hand stitching creates the neck shape (Fig. 173b).

5. Pad stitch the fall of the collar following its bias grain (Fig. 173c). These stitches are "easy" to permit the bias cut to ease around the neck and shoulders. Note again, that the direction and tension of the hand stitching creates the appropriate outside curve of the collar.

Here is another example: ZIPPER INSERTION

Many zippers are inserted in curved seams, the side seam of a skirt being the most familiar. The degree of this curve makes the seam bias or near bias. Machine stitching this stretchy area often results in a rippling seam, pulled out of shape. Hand stitching avoids this by putting the sewer in control.

Insert the zipper by either the regulation or slot-seam construction. Holding the zipper in the curve it will assume on the body (determined by your fitting of the seam), pin it to position and backstitch (or half backstitch, if you prefer). The result is a zippered seam that fits to perfection.

Hand stitching not only gives the sewer control of her stitching but gives her the opportunity for shaping she would find impossible with machine stitching.

A Fitting Close—a Closing That Fits

It is amazing how many garments would fit better if buttons, hooks and eyes, and snaps were properly placed and correctly sewn.

Buttons should be placed so that the garment does not pop open at the bust or gap at the waist. If for design reasons, buttons are not used at these two places, then the garment should be held closed with snaps covered to match the garment in color.

Buttons are sewed to the left front directly on the center line. Pin the garment closed (preferably over a slightly curved surface) matching the center markings—front or back, top and bottom. Using a safety pin (this won't fall out as a straight pin may) pin through the opening of the first buttonhole directly on the center line where the button is to be located. Close the safety pin. "Unbutton" the pin. Sew on the button. Button the garment.

Locate the position of the second button in the same way as the first. Sew on the second button. Repeat the procedure for the rest of the buttons. This method should make for a perfect closing.

HOW TO SEW ON THE BUTTON

If the button has a shank (Fig. 174a) take enough stitches through it to fasten the button securely. If the button has no shank you must create a stem with thread (Fig. 174b).

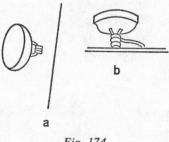

Fig. 174

The shank or stem is the bridge between the right and left front. It should be as long as the several layers of fabric are thick—outer fabric, interfacing, facing. The shank floats the button on the surface of the right front. Without it, the garment would bunch rather than button.

HOW TO SEW ON SNAPS

Mark the placement of the snaps to maintain a true lap. Sew the ball on first using a single thread. Sew with overhand stitches through the small holes at the edge (Fig. 175a). The stitches do not come through to the right side. Press the ball against the opposite edge to locate the exact position of the socket. Center the snap over the marking.

HOW TO SEW ON HOOKS AND EYES

Mark the position for the hooks and eyes carefully. Set the hook close to the edge of the garment for a true closing. Use straight eyes where the edges overlap (Fig. 175b). Use round eyes where the edges

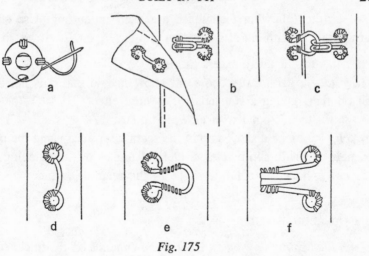

Fig. 175

meet (Fig. 175c). For this latter type of closing, extend the eye slightly beyond the edge. Sew the hook first. Sew the eye directly opposite it. Because there is considerable strain on hooks and eyes, sew them securely through the loops and around the bill of the hook (Figs. 175d, e, f).

To Look Trim—Trim!

If you want your garment to look trim—trim! The scissors is a liberator. It frees the seam or dart to do the shaping it was intended to do.

Some sewers are slash happy. They are fast on the draw. They'll cut anything—down to the stitching (sometimes to their dismay). Others are so fearful of the finality of cutting, they tremble to put scissors to cloth lest they commit some fatal error. Of course it is wise not to cut off any material until you are sure it fits you for size. When you have that certainty, cut off anything that restricts the fit. Once you've stitched the seams on the lines determined by the fitting, who needs *all* that stuff on the inside. It only makes for lumps, bumps, and strain. Cut it out!

All of the following techniques are used in cutting. Use small, sharp-pointed trimming scissors.

1. *trim*—to cut away excess fabric
2. *grade*—to trim away one seam allowance so that it is narrower than another, giving a staggered or layered effect
3. *slash*—to cut open with a sweeping stroke
4. *clip*—to make a short snip in the seam allowance using the point of a pair of small, sharp scissors at right angles to the stitching line
5. *notch*—to cut a small V-shape in the seam allowance

TRIM TO REDUCE BULK

Trim the Seam Allowances: How much depends on the thickness of the fabric—lightweight fabric requires less width than heavy fabric. Very sheer or transparent material that doesn't ravel may be trimmed back to the stitching line.

When seam allowances are to be pressed to one side, they must be *graded* to prevent bulk (Fig. 176a). Trim each seam allowance to a slightly different width. This applies to as many layers of fabric as are stitched into any one seam.

Trim all cross seams before stitching (Fig. 176h).

Grade the Seam Allowances of the Hem to the fold line to reduce bulk in a hem (Fig. 176i).

To Reduce Bulk Where a Pleat Enters a Hem: Clip at the top of the hem, press the graded seam allowances to one side, trim and press open the hem seam allowances (Fig. 176j).

To Free a Corner of Excess Bulk: Make three slashes—one diagonally across the corner, a second diagonally further into the seam allowance on one side, a third diagonally into the seam allowance on the other side. Cut close to the stitching line (Figs. 176k and 176 l).

Slash the Darts Open: Unless very narrow, darts in wool are always slashed open. Darts in soft silks and cottons need not be slashed open; they are pressed to one side.

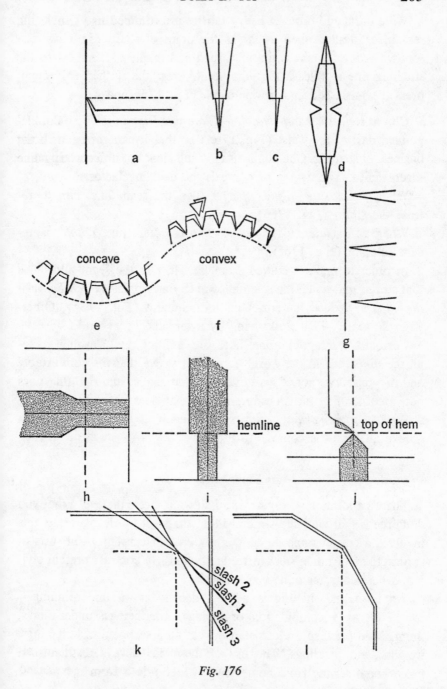

Fig. 176

Wide darts and darts in heavy fabrics are trimmed to ½ inch, the remainder slashed open as far as the point of sharp trimming scissors will go. Snip across the unslashed end of the dart almost to the stitching line to release the dart point. Press the slashed dart open; press the unslashed end to one side (Figs. 176b and c).

Clip to Release Strain—Notch to Eliminate Rippling: Clip a double-pointed dart at the waist (Fig. 176d) so that it can get on with the business of shaping. One clip is usually sufficient but if necessary make several clips. The degree of curve is the deciding factor.

When an *outside edge is shorter* than the seam line, *clip* to release the strain (Fig. 176e).

When an *outside edge is longer* than the seam line, *notch* to prevent rippling (Fig. 176f).

In order to make a curved seam lie flat, clip the seam allowance that strains and notch the seam allowance that ripples. *Notch between the clips* to reduce the strain on the stitching (Fig. 176g). Otherwise the seam will literally hang by a thread.

Correct trimming, clipping, notching, grading, and slashing makes all the difference in the world between a sleeve that fits comfortably and one that does not, a waistline dart that shapes and one that does not, a corner that turns easily and one that does not. The *trimming scissors is an important fitting tool*. Keep it at hand when sewing. Above all have the courage to use it.

More Than Meets the Eye

There's a lot more to a garment than what meets the eye! What you don't see is that vital sub-structure that shapes it up. In ages past this involved a considerable amount of undercover carpentry—all sorts of contraptions of bone, steel, wire, and wood. By contrast present styling is heroically restrained.

Yet its subtle shaping is no less dependent on underpinnings—some, all, or a combination of facings, interfacings, underlinings, linings, and often special assistance from an assortment of stiffenings, weights, and paddings. The use of these has always distinguished professional sewing from home sewing, high-priced from inexpensive ready-to-wear.

There are no hard and fast rules as to which interfacing or underlining should be used for a fabric. Choose that which will best produce and maintain the lines of the design. There are two guides—the design of the garment and the fabric used for it.

Any fabric will work as a supporting fabric for another. Here is a great chance to use up those odd pieces of organza, organdy, taffeta, broadcloth, lawn, or whatever else in that bulging drawer you hadn't the heart to throw away. Now available also are a great variety of commercial fabrics designed especially as shaping fabrics. There is such a bewildering array of these fabrics and each makes such extravagant claims about its superior qualities that it is often hard to make a choice.*

Each supporting fabric possesses special qualities. Each is meant to produce a special effect. The same material may be used on a variety of fabrics. A particular fabric may take any one of a number of shaping fabrics. In shopping for supporting fabric it is a good idea to take along a sample of the outer fabric. Drape it over the shaping material. You can then judge whether that particular support is what you want for this particular fabric. Remember—the determining factors are always the lines of the design and the fabric used for it.

So many terms are used in connection with the sub-structure that one can be easily confused. The names are really quite descriptive.

A *facing* is a finish for an outside edge. When the edge is curved, the facing is a separate piece curved to match and stitched to the outside edges of the garment. When the edge is straight the facing is generally turned up as a hem.

All outside edges of a garment—straight or curved—are subject to stress and wear. To reinforce these areas and strengthen them, the garment needs an *interfacing,* too. As its name implies, this is a supporting fabric placed *between* the *facing* and the *outer fabric.* In tailoring, this is often extended to include some shaping at the shoulder, chest, and even, in some instances, the bust and hips. Interfacing materials are generally compatible in weight with the fabric that they are interfacing, that is, lightweight interfacing for lightweight fabrics,

---

* A complete list of shaping materials useful in making a selection will be found in *The Complete Book of Tailoring* by this author, published by Doubleday & Co.

medium-weight interfacing for medium-weight fabrics, heavy interfacing for heavy fabrics.

An *underlining* is a shaping material cut from the same pattern pieces as the outer fabric and used to back it. For this reason it is often called a *backing*. By the use of an underlining one creates a new fabric with the surface appearance of the original fabric but the character of the underlining. For instance, let us say, you love the frosted look of chiffon. You would like to use it uncharacteristically—as a sheath. Obviously that fragile, limp chiffon by itself will never make it. So you add a crepe backing to create a new fabric—crepe-backed chiffon, which now can be used as you desire it. Underlinings may be any weight, texture, or crispness capable of producing the effect one has in mind.

Lining is a *cover-up*. It is used to hide the inner workings of the garment. To provide the right amount of ease and to accommodate any slight changes made in the fitting, the lining is stitched by machine separate from the garment and inserted by hand. Lining materials are generally of silk or fine cotton so that the garment is easy to slide into.

The lining material being different in character from the outer fabric will "hang out" differently. Stitching the two together may mean trouble. They are best treated independently of each other. This is particularly true for hems.

An *interlining* is a layer of cloth placed *between* the *outer fabric* and the *lining*. It is used for adding warmth to a coat or suit. Most frequently used is lamb's wool but chamois, outing flannel, or wool-backed satin are all also effective.

While there are technical differences in function between a lining, a backing, an interfacing, in truth there is a good deal of duplication. A lining provides more body for the outer fabric thereby helping to shape it. In doing so, it serves as a backing. A dress underlined in China silk has the feel of a lining. A lining or underlining joined at the outside edges reinforces and finishes those edges performing the role of facing and interfacing. An interlining used to add warmth to coat or suit also acts as a backing. Anything one puts under the outer fabric adds warmth.

Sometimes several different kinds of shaping materials are used in one garment—each performing a specific function in a particular part of the garment. Often an entire shell composed of several different supporting fabrics is placed under the outer fabric to shape and support it.

And if this is not enough, there is also a wide assortment of pads, ribbons, tapes, boning, wiring, weights, chains, and stiffenings that can also be used to fill out, stay put, hold up, or hold down any part of a garment to guarantee its shape.

FOR FILLING OUT

There are many standard pads commercially available for filling out and propping up all manner of curves and contours at shoulder, bust, or hips, for set-in sleeves, for kimono and raglan sleeves. As with all standard items, they may be tailored to suit—trimmed down, some of the stuffing removed, adjusted for individual needs.

Where unusual shaping is involved, appropriate padding can be made from the garment pattern. Often the dress or coat or suit pattern will contain a special pattern for the padding. There are many materials available by the yard which may be used for this purpose.

FOR HOLDING UP

Most garments hang from the shoulders but strapless or décolleté gowns must be supported from below. Long-ago styles used whalebone for this purpose. We use a more comfortable substitute—featherboning. Featherboning is used wherever the lines of a garment require a more definite shape and a more rigid support than that provided by underlining. The muslin-encased featherbone may be bought by the yard.

Also useful for the above purpose are

ribbonzene—muslin-encased twin wires available by the yard
zigzag wires—available in 3- to 4-inch lengths
white, enameled steel bones (the kind used for corsets or stays)
    that are $\frac{1}{4}$ inch wide and come in any required length

FOR HOLDING DOWN

You can't depend on gravity alone to hold a hem in place. If a hem is not sufficiently weighted, the entire garment has a tendency to ride up, displacing the seams and darts. For this reason, many hems (which are in reality facings) are interfaced. If the garment is backed, the underlining is turned up with the hem. If there is no underlining, the hem is interfaced with an appropriate material. In laces and sheer materials that have no hems, horsehair braid is used.

For spot weighting use lead weights—small disks that come in $\frac{5}{8}$- to $1\frac{1}{2}$-inch diameters.

For uniform weighting use weighted tapes of $\frac{1}{4}$-inch flat lead weights. Or, you may use lengths of muslin-enclosed shot put, the kind used for weighting drapes.

Any of the above weights may be used for holding cowls and other drapery in place.

Chanel made popular the chain weight stitched quite brazenly and openly to the top of the hem, the ends tucked under the facing. Such chains come in light and heavy weights, in brass or silver-colored metal. They are generally available in 24-inch pieces but some dressmaker and tailoring supply stores carry them by the yard.

TO STAY PUT

Designs with fullness (drapes, cowls, shirring, localized pleating, or gathering) generally call for a lining stay to keep the fullness in its rightful place. The stay is cut to fit the basic un-full shape of the garment or, sometimes, to fit the body. The fullness is stitched or tacked to this undercover control.

The waistline can be fixed for size and held in place with cotton tape, seam binding, or narrow ribbon stitched into the waistline seam. For a trim waistline in a fitted dress that has no waistline seam (sheath or princess styles), tack 1-inch grosgrain ribbon or stiff belting to all seams and darts at the waistline. The stay is cut to the exact length of the waistline. It fits particularly well if the ribbon is swirled into a waistline curve with the steam iron.

Lingerie strap guards hold the shoulders of a dress in place and keep the lingerie straps from peeping out. Use narrow ribbon, seam binding, or thread loops. Sew one end to the shoulder seam toward the sleeve edge, leaving the end toward the neck free to snap. Make the strap about 1½ inches or just long enough to enclose the lingerie straps comfortably. Sew the ball of the snap to the strap, the socket to the neck edge of the garment.

When it comes to sustaining the shape of fashion—anything goes!

The Sewer's Secret or What Goes on Under Cover of Cloth

To paraphrase one of the more popular ads, "Does she or doesn't she? Only the dressmaker knows for sure." What goes on under the surface of a beautiful garment must forever remain the sewer's secret. The beholder must be kept unaware of the sub-structure that supports the lines of the design. This calls for special methods for stitching the darts and seams of interfacing and underlining to render them unnoticeable.

TO STITCH A SEAM IN INTERFACING OR UNDERLINING MATERIAL

1. Mark each seam line. (The easiest marking is made with dressmaker's carbon paper and tracing wheel. Check to see that the color does not show through the outer fabric.)
2. Lap one seam line over the other.
3. Run a double line of plain machine stitching (Fig. 177a) or a row of zigzag stitching (Fig. 177b) close to the line. If stitching is done by hand, use cross-stitches (Fig. 177c).
4. Trim away the seam allowances close to the stitching on both sides.

TO STITCH A DART IN THE INTERFACING OR UNDERLINING

1. Mark the dart.
2. Slash one dart leg to the dart point (Fig. 177d).
3. Lap the slashed edge over the other dart leg (Fig. 177e).

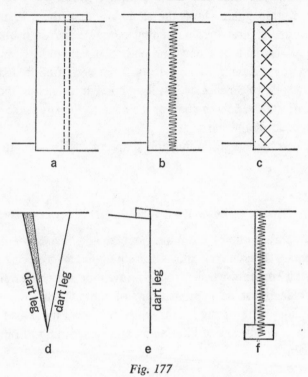

Fig. 177

4. Reinforce the point of the dart. Use a patch of muslin, tape, or interfacing material (Fig. 177f).

5. Stitch close to the cut edge. Use two lines of plain machine stitching, zigzag stitching, or cross-stitching.

6. Trim away the excess interfacing fabric on the underside close to the stitching.

In medium and heavyweight outer fabric and the same weight supporting fabric smoothest results are obtained when each is stitched separately, each pressed and blocked to shape, and then joined with tailor basting (Fig. 178b). The joining is done over the tailor's ham to simulate the curve of the body and to place both materials in the same relative position as they will be when worn. This is the order—ham (representing body), supporting fabric (shaded area), outer fabric (Fig. 178).

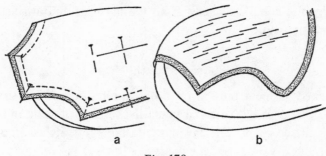

Fig. 178

In matching the outer and supporting fabrics start at the dart (Fig. 178a) and work toward the outer edges. When matching shaping seams, start at the crest of each curve and work toward the outer edges. You can see how this procedure makes for accurate shaping.

In Sheer or Lightweight Outer Fabric and Supporting Fabric, the following method of application may be used.

1. Cut the outer fabric and the underlining from the same pattern.
2. Transfer the pattern markings to the underlining.
3. Tailor-baste or stay stitch the fabrics together.
4. Stitch through the center of the dart joining both thicknesses.
5. Fold the dart on the stitching line, smoothing the underlining material in place.
6. Pin and stitch the dart through both thicknesses taking great care as the stitching comes off the dart point.

Whenever possible, stitch the darts separately for a smoother effect.

While supporting materials may be stitched into the major construction seams, hair canvas never is. It is too resilient to press flat. Trim away the seam allowance of the hair canvas. Slip the trimmed edge of the canvas under the seam allowance to the seam line. It may be fastened in place in either one of two ways:

1. Catch stitch the canvas to the outer fabric with tiny, invisible stitches.
2. Catch stitch the seam allowance to the canvas.

Linings are completed apart from the garment and attached to it with slip stitching.

Press for Permanent Shape

A shaped garment pressed on a flat ironing board? Doesn't seem quite logical, does it? You find yourself carefully pressing out of the garment all the shape you have so painstakingly stitched into it.

It is true that your garment will assume some of the contours of your body in wearing partly because your 98° temperature does some blocking to shape. But, you cannot wait until your project is complete and rely on nature to do the blocking for you. Pressing is as important to the construction of your garment as the sewing is. The greatest sewing in the world looks unfinished and amateurish if unpressed. What is even more important, the garment will never fit as was intended.

TO GET THE GREATEST FITTING BENEFIT FROM THE STITCHING:

1. Press every dart and seam before stitching it to a cross seam.
2. Press and shape each unit before joining it to another.
3. Press open all enclosed seams before turning to the right side.
4. Press all edges when turned.
5. Turn under the seam allowance and press to shape before inserting a zipper.
6. Turn up and press the hem easing the raw edge as much as necessary, to make it lie flat before adding the binding and attaching the hem.
7. Press seam allowances in the direction that produces least bulk.
8. When an uncut dart in outer fabric falls directly over an uncut dart in a lining, press each in a different direction.

And, speaking of bulk, keep the trimming scissors handy. Clip or notch wherever needed to make the seam or dart lie flat. Slash and grade to remove every last little bit of bulk.

CAUTION: Never press a dart or seam open or press a crease in anything until you are certain of its fit. It is too difficult—in some cases, impossible—to press out the crease.

PRESSING IS DONE WITH HEAT, MOISTURE, PRESSURE, PROTECTION

The amount of each depends on the fabric. Use a safe heat setting
on the iron. Use just the amount of moisture necessary. For some
fabrics you will not use any and for others even the steam iron is not
enough. For the latter, create your own moist heat with a damp cloth
and a dry iron. Some fabrics are pounded flat, while others would be
ruined by this treatment. Provide whatever protection is necessary for
the fabric. It is wise to test press a dart or seam in a scrap of your
material to determine the best treatment for it.

PRESS PADS

Except for long, flat seams *all pressing is done over shaped press
pads.* There is enough variety in the shape of these numerous pads to
accommodate all known curves. However, the most all-around useful one is the tailor's ham. This is indispensable for tailoring and
every bit as useful in dressmaking. There are tailor's hams commercially available but they are really quite easy to make.

How to Make a Tailor's Ham. Cut out and stitch together two egg-
shaped bias pieces of heavy, firmly woven cloth to the dimensions
given in Fig. 179a. Dart the broader end for more shaping. Machine
stitch the two thicknesses of cloth leaving the broader end open. *Pack
very tightly* with hardwood sawdust until the ham is quite hard; it
cannot do its shaping unless it is. Slip stitch the open end.

Use silesia, duck, drill, unbleached muslin, or any similar firm cot-

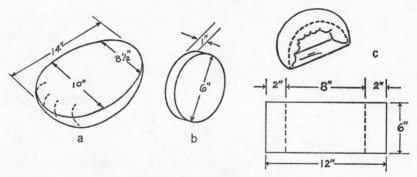

Fig. 179

Fig. 179

ton. The commercial ones are made of firmly woven woolens, which can also be used for yours. Hams may be stuffed with cotton waste, with old nylon stockings, or with wool scraps. Sawdust has the merit of absorbing moisture more quickly and more effectively. Since drying to shape is very much a part of the blocking process this absorptiveness is an important quality for a press pad to possess.

The following areas are always pressed and blocked over some curved press pad: all bodice darts and control seams; all skirt darts and control seams; all shaped side seams and underarm sections; all waistline seams; all shoulder and elbow ease or shoulder and elbow darts; all sleeve caps; all collars and lapels; all hips of skirts and jackets.

In addition, block the in-depth shape of all areas that go over or around some part of the body. Starting at center front or center back, press toward the outer edges all necklines, shoulders, armholes, all underarm sections of bust, waist, hips (Fig. 180). Even a no-dart garment can have some shape blocked into it in this way.

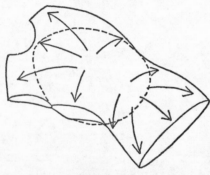

Fig. 180

In pressing over the tailor's ham, place the shaped area over the ham on a curve that best corresponds to the curve of the garment. The right side of the fabric is against the ham, the wrong side up. Pressing is always done on the wrong side. This procedure produces a reverse curve temporarily. When the seam or dart has been pressed open, turn the garment to the right side over the tailor's ham. Steam press the shaped area protecting the fabric as necessary.

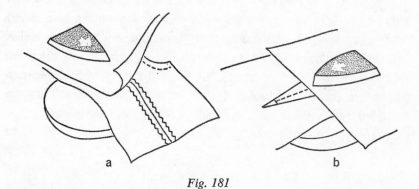

a   b

Fig. 181

Press with the lengthwise grain in the direction of the stitching (Fig. 181a). In pressing a dart, place the dart over a corresponding curve of the tailor's ham and press from the wide end to the dart point (Fig. 181b). Use a light rotary motion at the dart point to smooth out the "bump" when necessary. Sometimes it is even necessary to pull the fabric taut while pressing to round off the bulge produced by the dart. However you do it, make certain that the dart point blends perfectly into the fabric and that the entire area is smoothly curved.

To guarantee the permanent contour of the garment, block the interfacing and underlining in exactly the same way before joining them to the outer fabric.

COLLAR SHAPING

Always in tailoring and often in dressmaking, *collars and set-in sleeves* are *blocked to shape before being stitched into place.*

The *collar can be shaped* over a curve of the tailor's ham. A rolled

Turkish towel curved into a horseshoe shape is a simple device if there is no press pad. Designed especially for collar shaping are the collar press board (Fig. 179b) and the collar press pad (Fig. 179c).

The *collar press board* is a circle of hardwood 6 inches in diameter and 1 inch thick.

A *collar press pad* can be made of the same materials as the tailor's ham cut to the same dimensions as the collar press board.

Fig. 179c is a *press pad* equally useful *for pressing collars and sleeve caps*. It is easy to use slipped over the narrow end of a sleeve board. To make the pad cut a bias strip of heavy cotton 6 inches wide by 12 inches long. Fold this rectangle lengthwise and stitch the long side. Press and turn inside out. Stuff it tightly with sawdust to within 2 inches of each end and hand stitch across the pad. Turn the unstuffed 2-inch ends under to fit the sleeve board. Overlap and stitch them securely to each other.

How to Press a Collar to Shape: Following is the method used in tailoring. Adapt as much of this technique as you can for dressmaking. This will depend largely on the fabric used.

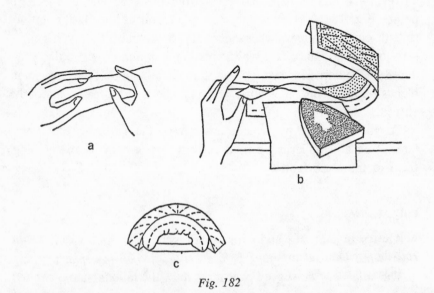

Fig. 182

1. Apply the interfacing to the undercollar. Pad stitch to position. The burden of the collar shaping is borne by the undercollar.

2. Fold the collar along the roll line (Fig. 182a).

3. Steam the stand of the undercollar in an inside curve (Fig. 182b).

4. Place the collar over the collar press pad (or board) (Fig. 182c).

5. Steam the fall of the collar to shape while in position on the press pad. Do not press a crease in the roll line. The collar must *roll* along this line.

6. Let the collar dry naturally while on the press pad.

7. Remove the undercollar from the press pad and apply the upper collar remembering to stitch in such manner that the neck shape is preserved.

8. Mold the completed collar into neck shape and steam press.

9. Pin to position on any of the shaping devices and allow the collar to dry in shape. The neck of your dress form is a perfect place for this last shaping bit. Then you will be sure that the collar will fit you.

10. When dry, attach the collar to the garment.

LAPEL SHAPING

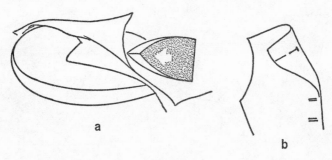

Fig. 183

Since a lapel lies over the curve of the chest, press it over a suitable curve of the tailor's ham (Fig. 183a). While it is still damp, *roll* the lapel to position. Allow it to dry on the ham.

It is a good idea to pin the lapel to position while drying. Do not press a crease in the roll line. The lapel must *roll* on the roll line.

The lapel, too, is pressed to shape both during construction and when completed.

PRESS PADS USEFUL FOR SLEEVE SHAPING

Any of these press pads can be used for shrinking and shaping the sleeve cap; the narrow end of the tailor's ham, the broad end of the sleeve board (Fig. 179d), the press mitt (Fig. 179e), a sleeve press pad (Fig. 179f).

How to Shape the Sleeve Cap of a Set-in Sleeve: This method is recommended only for those fabrics that can take steam. The cap of the sleeve is blocked to fit over the curve of the shoulder and provide ease of movement.

METHOD I—*the most usual method*

1. Stitch the sleeve seam and press it open on a sleeve board.

2. Place two rows of gathering—hand or machine—across the cap. Draw up the gathering, distributing the fullness evenly.

3. Slip the sleeve over the press pad, wrong side up. Fit the cap over the pad.

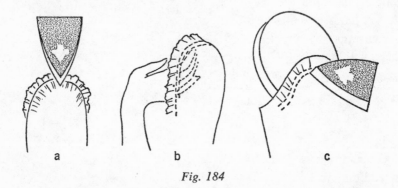

a   b   c

Fig. 184

4. Shrink out the fullness with the point of the steam iron (Fig. 184a). Gently push blocked cap to right side. You should be able to hold the cap with your hooked fingers (Fig. 184b).

METHOD II

1. Leave the sleeve seam unstitched.

2. Gather across the cap and draw up the gathers to cap shape. Distribute the fullness evenly.

3. Place the sleeve cap, wrong side up, over the tailor's ham.

4. Shrink out the fullness with the point of the steam iron (Fig. 184c). Reverse the curve to right side.

5. Stitch the sleeve seam and press it open.

Whichever of the above two methods you choose, the important thing is to shape the cap before the sleeve is set and stitched into the armhole. For one thing it is much easier to do the shaping before setting the sleeve than after. For another, it makes the sleeve setting itself much simpler. With the cap ease disposed of the seam line of the sleeve now matches the seam line of the armhole.

That pressing-to-shape improves the appearance of a garment is without question. That it improves the fit of a garment may come as a revelation.

Store in Shape

Once the darts and shaping seams have been stitched and once the garment has been pressed and blocked to shape, it would be folly to store it flat between sewing sessions. Why lose that beautiful shaping?

Hang up each pressed and blocked part of the garment. Stuff to shape with tissue paper. Best of all, pin each section to shape on your dress form.

The Proof of the Sewing Is in the Fitting

Often problems in fitting are in reality problems in construction. In addition to your fitting skills, you must develop wisdom in the choice of supporting fabric, precision in stitching, courage in cutting, a sculptural hand in pressing. Everything one does in construction contributes not only to the beauty of the garment but to its beautiful fit.

Chapter VIII

AN EYE FOR FASHION FITTING

HOW TO CHOOSE A STYLE WITH AN EYE TO ITS FITTING POTENTIAL

It's that time of year! (When isn't it?) And though spring, summer, autumn, winter are not nearly over, we are leaping ahead to the new season. What to wear? What to make? What to buy? The newspapers and magazines are full of absorbing disclosures of what's new in Paris, Rome, London, New York, or wherever. The accompanying photographs and sketches reveal who's showing what and who's wearing which. We're off! The dreaming and the scheming have begun.

In looking at fashions, most women lose all sense of objectivity. They "luv-v-v" this or that according to the image they have of themselves in it. When a style doesn't fit into their very own formula for glamor they are apt to discard it with unkind words. Consciously or unconsciously, we are all looking for only that newness which can bring some beauty to the bodies we are stuck with. The search is constant.

There is a popular theory that some designers create their unshapely fashions because they hate women. What is more probable is that a couturier reacts as any other artist reacts to a blank area that cries out for design. Given the present state of art, a dress is just as likely to end up "abstract" design as a canvas is. The fact that eventually a body will wind up under the abstraction is almost incidental. Many a dress designer is perfectly willing to sacrifice the woman for the work. This has more to do with his love of art than his hatred of women. On the other hand, there are always those great mechanics who design and build solid-enough structures—completely uninspired. You'll find both such types of clothes in the pattern books and on the ready-to-wear racks.

There is a happy mean that combines beautiful design with essential structure. Many intriguing designs cleverly incorporate into their style lines all the opportunities one needs to make for flattering fit. The trick is to find *the* design with the greatest potential for your figure.

The following discussion uses for illustration styles that are currently fashionable. Considering the life expectancy of a book vis-à-vis fickle fashion, this is a risky thing to do at any time. It is particularly so at this moment—when fashion appears to be on the verge of one of those major cyclical upheavals. If the reader will think in terms of categories of fitting problems rather than of specific style lines, this hazard can be overcome. On the positive side, it is the author's hope that this method of illustration will vividly pinpoint the possibilities for fitting that appear in clothing designs.

Inventory—Assets, Liabilities

First off, one must recognize that some styles are just not meant for some figures. This calls for an honest stock-taking of figure assets and liabilities and very strict discipline when it comes to choice of designs. Sure it takes a hard heart and iron will to turn a deaf ear to all the goodies the columnists and ad writers constantly entice you with but if you know a style is not for you, avoid it like the plague.

Your past successes and past failures can be excellent guides in choosing styles that are becoming to you. However, don't be so glued to those dreamy things you wore once upon a time that you shy away from trying what's new and fresh. You may not want to be among the first to hop on the bandwagon of a new fashion but don't wait to be the last holdout. You'll get a lot more mileage out of your clothes if you latch on to an incoming fashion rather than finally adopting an outgoing one.

Shape with Bias

For natural shaping, nothing is better than bias. Of itself, it molds, it clings, it moves, it defines. It is a style eminently suited to a flat-chested, slim-hipped era. That is why it is used so much today. (It was equally popular in the twenties, another such era, when Vionnet first used bias cut for her dresses.)

For undeveloped figures, bias provides sufficient shaping without the use of darts or control seams. For developed figures, such designs at best provide inadequate shaping and at worst can be downright disastrous.

The dress in Fig. 185a depends for its fit on its bias cut. The only seams which could possibly be used for shaping are at the side, the

Fig. 185

center front, the center back, and the raglan sleeve. At that, the amount of possible fitting in these places is minimal. There is no provision for shaping in the bust area. Should one wish to use this design for a full-bosomed figure, one would have to create a bodice-front dart. A French underarm dart that repeated the line of the raglan sleeve would be a possibility but there is enough happening in the design already (collar, raglan sleeve, front tab, buttons, welt, and front pleat) without the addition of a dart line.

The dress in Fig. 185b depends on its bias bodice and its vertical

Fig. 185

style lines for fit. The latter are too far off the bust and too far off the shoulder blades to be used for shaping. This is a great and interesting design for one who needs little shaping.

Fig. 185c does have some shaping features as part of its design: the neckline fullness and the French underarm dart. It has certain other hazards, however. The unrestricted movement characteristic of bias tends to reveal every body curve even in semifitted dresses like this one. To counteract this, bias clothes should be fitted with more-than-usual ease (Fig. 185d).

Fig. 186

When a cowl or other drapery is part of a design, the fabric must be cut on the bias to provide the drape. In Fig. 186a the entire dress is bias cut. Drapability for the cowl—yes, but also figure-revealing shape for the rest of the dress. To avoid this the bias often is confined to the cowl (Fig. 186b) or to the bodice (Fig. 186c). The rest of the garment may then be cut on the safer straight grain.

Because bias can be so beautifully molded and shaped to fit, it is often used for sleeves and collars.

Fig. 186

When a sleeve is cut on the bias (Fig. 187a) it is comparatively easy to block into a cap and set. Bias sleeves have a wonderful easy movability. They "give" with every motion of the arm.

The standing (turtleneck) collar in Fig. 187a is cut on the bias to shape around the neck.

The undercollar of the classic tailored, set-on, notched collar (Fig. 187b) is always cut on the bias. This makes it possible to pad stitch and block the collar into a neck shape.

You can expect bias-cut garments to stretch and dip on hanging out. That is the nature of bias and there is nothing you can do to

Fig. 187

prevent it. However, you can minimize the problems this presents by letting the fabric sections hang out after cutting and before stitching. (You will find that a dart stitched before the fabric is stabilized will drop from the desired position in the settling process.) The amount of time it takes to stabilize a bias-cut fabric depends on the size and the heaviness of the piece. To prevent stretching after the garment is completed, store it flat. (Incidentally, all of the above is also true of knitted fabrics. They should be treated like bias.)

Bias cut calls for a complete pattern. (Half a pattern on a fold of bias fabric is as easy to cut as Jell-O.) It takes considerably more

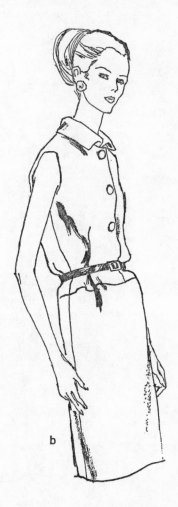

a   b

Fig. 188

material. It requires expertise in cutting, stitching, pressing, and fitting. All this makes for limited use despite the drapability of bias, its ease of movement, its effortless shaping, its gracefulness.

Safe, Straight Grain

Most garments are cut on the safe, straight grain with or without dart control. The "with dart control" is for the shapely figures; the "without dart control" must be reserved for the girlish (or boyish) figures.

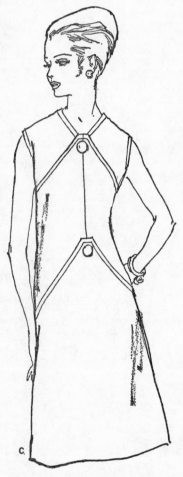

Fig. 188

While Fig. 188a has no darts, some slight shaping is achieved on the side seams. Its semifittedness provides enough encompassing fabric for a slight figure but not nearly enough to accommodate an ample or mature one.

The fullness of Fig. 188b reduces the amount of shaping necessary. In this design, rather minimal dart control is evident in the fold at the waistline held in place by the narrow belt.

Some fitting could be done at the center front and -back seams of Fig. 188c—but not much. The topstitched bodice seaming is placed a little too high to be useful for shaping. Were it lowered sufficiently,

Fig. 189

it could function as a control seam. This would, however, disturb the fine proportion and delicate balance of the three sections.

Take Heart—Create a Dart

It is possible to create darts in a pattern that has none or too few. It is possible to convert existing darts into control seams. Any change that is made must be consistent with the original design.

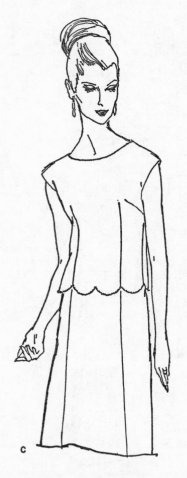

Fig. 189

The lines of the design in Fig. 189a would really not suffer too much (if any) by the creation of a small dart emerging from the side-front seam (Fig. 189b). Many designs are shaped in just this way.

The waistline dart of Fig. 189c can be extended to take care of narrow shoulders in a perfectly acceptable manner. In fact this is the line of the jacket (Fig. 189d).

Both vertical darts in the jacket of Fig. 189e can be extended to the hem the better to fit narrow hips (Fig. 189f).

e

Fig. 189

a   b

Fig. 190

All of the dresses in Fig. 190 have good control in their darts, seams, and fullness. On the whole, this ABC sort of fit is not nearly as interesting as the more complex designs. Whatever charm these designs possess (and they do) lies in their other style details or in the use of beautiful fabric.

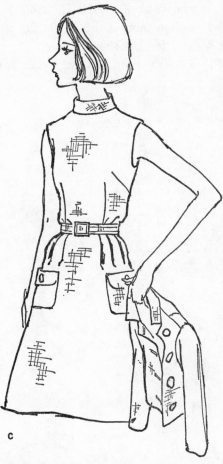

c

Fig. 190

Additional Fullness

In many a garment, the shaping is concealed in its fullness. It may not be visible and it may not be much, but it is there. Sometimes fullness even covers up inadequacy of shaping but you cannot rely on this. Additional fullness is essentially decorative; shaping is structural. Any change in the fullness can affect the fit; any change in the fit must inevitably affect the fullness.

The gathers at the neckline of Fig. 191a create the shape for the bust as well as add design interest. More gathers are necessary for more shape, less gathers for less shape.

The pleats in Fig. 191b taper up to a fitted yoke at the hips provid-

Fig. 191

ing movement without bulk. Changes in fit should be made proportionately on all the pleats as well as the skirt yoke.

The released tucks of Fig. 191c shape the bodice and add fullness below. Since there are so many tucks, a bit of fitting could be done on each.

c

Fig. 191

Some garments are so full that their no-shape does for all shapes. This is so whether the garment is unbelted (Fig. 191d) or belted (Fig. 191e).

d

Fig. 191

Fig. 191

The Princess Line

The true princess style is fitted. In one style line it is possible to fit shoulders, chest, bust, waist, and hips. How can you beat that? No wonder the princess style remains perennially popular even in less fitted and modified versions.

Fig. 192a—the semifitted princess-style dress and jacket. The lines of the dress speak for themselves. Horizontal seaming across the bust

Fig. 192

of the jacket gives an additional seam that can be used for fitting. (Fitting can be horizontal as well as vertical.)

Fig. 192b—a modified princess. The H-seaming provides an across-the-bust seam for additional fitting.

Fig. 192c—a modified princess style with seaming that emerges from the armhole, an excellent fitting line for a narrow-chested, full-busted figure.

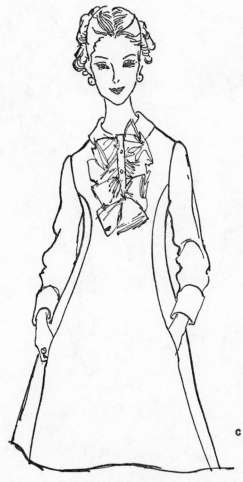

Fig. 192

Yokes and Insets

Yokes and insets whose seam lines fall across the bust or shoulder blades give excellent opportunities for fitting.

Fig. 193a—the front and back bib-like insets of this design place the seaming where it can be used for fitting—over the bust, over the shoulder blades.

Fig. 193

Fig. 193b—the shaping in this dress is deceptive. The yoke appears to be there merely to provide color contrast. In reality, the seam line falling across the bust is a control seam excellent for fitting this otherwise unfitted dress.

Fig. 193c—the Y-shaped front yoke plus the A lines of the dress afford many places where this dress can be fitted.

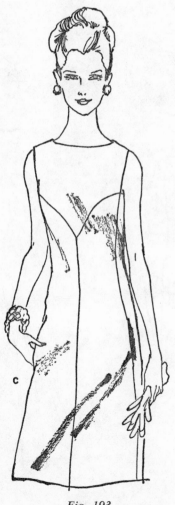

Fig. 193

Combinations

Many designs utilize *combinations* of yokes, darts, tucks, pleats, gathers, control seams, style lines, etc., as several places in a garment where fitting can be done.

Fig. 194a—control seams, ease of bodice, fullness of skirt.

Fig. 194b—control seams of bodice, pleats of skirt.

Fig. 194

Fig. 194c—center-front and -back seams, side seams, waistline darts, front and back, dart tucks at neck.

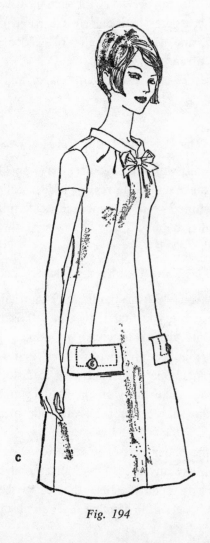

Fig. 194

Late-blooming Beauties

Relaxed dresses are wonderful for day-time activities. Somehow, when evening comes, a woman longs to be feminine and seductive. To her, this means a fit that closely follows the lines of her body—particularly the bust. Standard gear is a gown with great exposure that fits the bosom with great art.

Think of the bust as a small hemisphere and you will understand the principle of the shaping necessary for such fit. It is best exemplified in the shaping of brassieres, particularly the wired ones: seams that cut under, around, and across the half-globe aided by darts shaped like the segments of an orange.

Fig. 195—unabashed sexiness in cut, shape, and exposure to be fitted accordingly.

The Easy Way Out Is Not Really

While a simple shift with one lone dart may appeal to you because it appears easy to make and fit, in reality, it does not provide as many opportunities for fitting as one with more intricate lines so placed that they can control the shaping.

Leave Well Enough Alone

When you select a style from the literally thousands that confront you, you do so because you find it pleasing. It is that because the designer used all his artistry to create its appeal: that enchanting color combination, that beautiful sweep of line, that delicate, just-right balance of all its parts. One would not want to distort or destroy this even in an effort to make the garment fit. If you tamper with the proportions and the shape, you must pit your artistry against the designer's.

In fitting, it is the better part of wisdom to *leave the focal points of interest alone*. Make any necessary changes above, below, beside, anywhere—but do not touch the lines that carry the design. Fitting can be done on that part of the garment that can absorb the change.

a   b

Fig. 195

In Fig. 196a it is possible to make the yoke slightly shorter or longer, narrower or wider but you would hardly want to change its intriguing shape. Though fitting must be done on the seam, change only that part of the dress below the yoke.

In Fig. 196b you would run into real trouble if you attempted to change the X-seaming and the front panel. The logical place to do the fitting is beside this intricate detail.

Fig. 196

In Fig. 196c it makes sense to fit the dress above and below the midsection and not alter by one tiny bit its size or shape. That band is what this dress is all about.

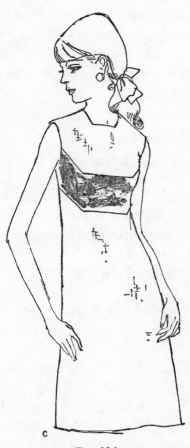

c

Fig. 196

Suggestions for Sewers

Look for those styles with lines or darts that can be manipulated to make the garment fit you. Remember that they must fall directly over or very close to the high points of the body.

Preserve the distinctive details that engaged your interest. Fit the garment only in places where the change can be absorbed without altering the salient style features.

Changes in style are possible. After all, even designers play with a theme and often produce variations of the same design. Were you one of their clients, they undoubtedly would make some changes for you. When a non-professional makes such changes, she must be guided by the same art principles and elements of design. A sleeve from this pattern, a collar from that one, this skirt with that bodice, can result in a hodgepodge if one is not extremely careful. It can be done—but it takes some doing!

Suggestions for Those Who Buy Their Clothes

If the clothes you buy need altering, all of the foregoing suggestions for sewers are equally valid for you plus a few additional ones.

One must determine whether modifications are possible to make the garment fit and just how much reconstruction is involved. One must also weigh the value of extensive alterations in work, expense, and ultimate result.

Non-sewers often have the most wildly improbable ideas of how much work is involved in an alteration. It's as if wishing could make it so—in an instant.

"How much work can there be to a simple hem?" Only yards of fabric, interfacing, machine work, handwork, finish.

"Why can't this dart be moved?" Only because it was slashed open at the factory and how can you move a slash!

"There's plenty of seam allowance. Why can't it be let out to make this size 8 fit me?" It can be if you like the line of decorative little needle holes left in the fabric when the stitching is removed.

"There's plenty of material. Can't you make it my size?" Yes, if you take the whole thing apart, recut it, reshape it, and restitch it.

"All it needs is a little lifting at the shoulders." Only! Take off the collar, the facings; remove the sleeves; take out the lining, interfacing, backing; recut the shoulders, neckline, armhole, sew and press the entire garment again. And, oh yes, what about that buttonhole—any chances of moving that?

The truth of the matter is that some alterations can't be done, and others shouldn't be done. It is often more work, more trouble, and more time-consuming to remake a garment than to make it in the first place. This is why alterations are so expensive and why it is difficult to find competent dressmakers to do the job.

If you still insist on having alterations done see the suggestions for sewers on page 248. In addition:

Look for uncut darts and ample seam allowances. Test a tiny area of the fabric in an inconspicuous place to see whether the removal of the stitching will leave needle marks. Consider how many parts of the garment must be taken apart, recut, and restitched.

From Fitting Potential to Fulfillment of Promise

A style with fitting potential may remain just that unless one knows how to cope with the problems (and opportunities) that arise from the design.

FITTING THE UNFITTED

The past decade has been a period of relatively unfitted clothing. But even the shiftiest of shift dresses needs some shaping. In every design, no matter how unfitted it appears to our eyes, there are points at which the fabric touches the body. This subtle fitting is often much more difficult to achieve than a more obvious fitted look.

Fig. 197

Consider these two unfitted dresses (Figs. 197a and b). Were you to cover up the lower portion of each of these dresses you might well think that the neckline, shoulders, chest, armscyes, and sleeve were those of a fitted dress. In Fig. 197a, there is even a bust dart that emerges from the armhole to fool you further. It is particularly important that these places be painstakingly fitted to make the dress say YOU. An indefinite fullness can cover anybody else as well.

Fig. 197

It is subtle fitting that distinguishes a beautifully fitted dress from a bag. (Remember all those unkind remarks about the "sack" when the skimmer dress was first introduced? It wasn't really accepted until its lines were brought under control by fitting that had some reference to the body.)

Figs. 197c and d require all the care one would lavish on a close-fitting dress.

Study these two new designs that hail the return of the fragile, feminine, and romantic look. (Farewell, Moon-maids. Hello, Milk-maids!) No fit (except at the waistline) is required of the full skirts, which cover a multitude of sins as well as shins. Such fitting as there is in these designs is concentrated in the bodice, at the neckline, shoulders, chest, bust, and waistline. Fig. 198a is quite fitted. Fig. 198b has considerable ease.

Fig. 198

From the standpoint of fitting, the one-piece sheath dress has much in common with the fitted-bodice, full-skirt style. The degree of fitting for both depends on the desired closeness to and definition of the body.

b

Fig. 198

CLOSED FOR FITTING

When a closure is involved in the design (Fig. 199a), it should be completed and closed before the garment can be fitted. In this dress (Fig. 199b), it is obvious that the band must be attached before fitting is even possible.

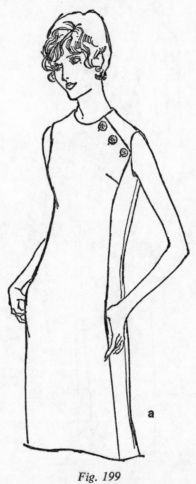

a

Fig. 199

When the garment is closed by a zipper, carefully pin fit the seam into which it will be inserted. As soon as the seam line is determined, either baste or permanently stitch in the zipper. This makes getting in and out of the garment so much easier for subsequent fittings.

Fig. 199

DON'T LET THE FULLNESS FOOL YOU

When tucks or pleats occur in a design as in Fig. 200a, they must be pinned or basted to position before the garment can be fitted. One must never depend on the opened pleat to provide extra fullness. To do so destroys the lines of the design.

The tucks originating at the bodice center front of Fig. 200b are designed to be on an angle and should be fitted so. If they veer off in any other direction, the bodice needs refitting. It would be wise to

Fig. 200

baste the tucks in place first and then handle the bodice as if it were a fitted one.

The gathers in Fig. 200c are planned to fall vertically from the diagonal seaming. They must not pull off at an angle. If they do, refit the lower part of the bodice. This may mean either redistributing the gathers or adding width. Be careful not to change the diagonal seam; this would destroy the uniqueness of this design. Check the skirt, too, for vertical fall of fullness. If correction is needed, treat the skirt in the same way as the bodice.

Fig. 200

Fig. 201

Skirt fullness across the abdomen is unflattering for any but a slim and absolutely flat figure. All others do well to redistribute the gathers so that the least fullness is at center front making the skirt fall flat against the body. In Fig. 201a note that the gathers have been pushed toward the side seams and kept minimal at the front. In Fig. 201b the front is flat while the pleats are located toward the side. The fullness in Fig. 201c will tend to make any figure look pregnant. (The Empire design was originally a maternity dress.) To redistribute the gathers in this dress would really spoil the design. There is something about the way it puffs out that is charming—if you have the figure for it.

c

Fig. 201

Localized fullness should be held in place by a stay. In Fig. 202a the gathered front neckline is so held. In Fig. 202b both the cowl and the fullness that drops from it are held in place by stays. In some cases, the lining can act as the stay (Fig. 202c).

Fig. 202

Gathering the lining as well as the outer fabric at the neckline will produce an undesirable bulkiness in any but very sheer material. To avoid this, cut an un-full lining or dart it to provide the dress shaping. Gather the outer fabric. Join the two.

In all of the above illustrations, the lining or the stay is fitted to the figure. The fullness is applied as a decorative feature.

Fig. 202

Take the Plunge

Décolleté necklines call for some anchor to hold them in place against the body.

The low V of the dress neckline in Fig. 203 should be anchored to the bra not only for the wearing but for the fitting as well. This anchor can be a covered hook of boning or zigzag wiring. One end is stitched to the point of the décolletage and the other hooked into the bra.

Fig. 203

A square décolletage can be held in place with a length of narrow elastic. It should be long enough to encircle the body from one corner of the neckline to the other. Sew one end against the neck facing close to the corner. Try on the dress. Bring the other end around the body snugly to the opposite corner. Mark the exact measurement. Remove the dress. Sew the ball of the snap to the free end; sew the socket to the facing as marked. A dress with a center opening has two ends instead of one. Fasten these with hook and eye under the dress closing.

Here is a way of guaranteeing that an off-the-shoulder neckline doesn't get out-of-bounds.

1. Make a thread casing with catch stitching wide enough to accommodate ¼ to ½ inch elastic. Place the casing just inside the arm-hole edge of the dress from the front notch (or its equivalent), over the shoulder, to the back notch.

2. Cut a length of elastic ½ to 1 inch shorter than the casing.

3. Pin one end of the elastic to the front edge, thread the elastic through the casing, and pin the other end to the back edge. Try on the dress. Adjust the elastic as necessary. When satisfied with the fit, sew both ends securely to position.

While this looks gathered off the person, the elastic stretches to fit snugly when the dress is worn.

Any device that you can invent or adopt to hold a neckline in place is legitimate.

That Wandering Waistline

Since that long-lost waistline has made its reappearance, like it or not we are all about to be involved with waistline fittings.

For a waistline to fit right it must be in the right place and in the right amount. See Chapter V for a full discussion of waistline fitting.

BRIEFLY, TO REFRESH YOUR MEMORY

The waistline of your dress may be where you want it to be rather than where nature placed it.

All waistlines are slightly curved. The "normal" waistline dips slightly toward the front. (Too much dip in front makes a figure look older or slightly pitched forward.) Some waistlines tilt backward (swayback).

A dress with a waistline seam (Fig. 204a) is fitted more snugly at the waist than a fitted dress without one. For instance, a princess-line dress (Fig. 204b) is indented at the natural waistline but never fits so tight that there is strain.

When a dress is belted, try on the dress with the belt for a fitting.

a   b

Fig. 204

Make sure that the waistline seam does not show. The belt is supposed to cover it.

In most skirts, the waistband fits the narrowest part of the waistline indentation. Therefore, it should be narrow—1 to 1¼ inches. Anything wider needs to be shaped to fit the curve.

Consider a ¾-inch waistband cut on the bias to rest snugly in the waistline without wrinkling. In reckoning its length, make an allowance for the stretch of the bias. The heavier the fabric and the wider the sweep of the skirt, the more pull is exerted on the waistband and

Fig. 205

the greater the stretch. Make this waistband 1 to 2 inches less than the actual waist measurement.

When seated the waistline is a larger measurement than when standing. If the waistline fits snugly when standing, be prepared for some discomfort when sitting. To avoid this some skirts are fitted in a slightly dropped position—1 inch below the natural waistline (Fig. 205a). Hip-huggers are most comfortable of all when sitting since there is no problem of shifting measurement and fit. (Did it ever occur to you

Fig. 205

that cowboys who sit in the saddle so much of the day wear hip-hugger pants for this reason?)

For most figures, skirts look best when the flare breaks at the upper hip rather than the waist (Fig. 205a). This makes for a smoother fit across the abdomen and hips. If you have any tendency to round-ness in this area, a skirt that flares from the waist will only accentu-ate it.

A hip yoke is a fine solution to this problem. Fig. 205b has a bias flared skirt that drops from a hip yoke.

In Fig. 205c, the flare starts at the lower hip.

Fullness or flare in a skirt may start any place that is flattering to the figure. This would be easy enough to control in a design such as Fig. 205d.

Collar Comfort

The presently popular collarless neckline is a difficult style for many women to wear. It calls for a firm chin, a smooth and slender neck, and a good set to the shoulders. For the rest of us, the severity of this neckline needs softening with those faithful pearls, a dashing scarf, or a flattering collar. A collar may seem a simple enough item but it has a number of working parts that determine its fit.

1. *The neckline:* This is the part of the collar that is stitched to the neckline of the garment. It may or may not match the garment in length and shape. Many collars today are set on dropped neck-lines. Even when a neckline is high, it should have sufficient ease to run your finger around it.

2. *The style line:* This is the outer edge of the collar. As with any other style line this may be anything the designer wishes it to be. The style line always falls on that part of the shoulders which equals it in circumference, pushing the rest of it into a stand. As the outer edge or circumference of the collar shortens, the stand increases. As the collar circumference increases, the stand decreases.

3. *The stand:* The stand of a collar is the amount of the rise from the neckline to the roll line. If you have a short neck, you should lower

the stand of the collar to make it comfortable for you. On the other hand, if you have a long neck, you could, if you wished, raise the stand.

4. *The roll line:* This is the line along which the collar turns down —when it does. A standing collar obviously has no roll line.

5. *The fall:* This is the depth of the collar from the roll line to the style line. It must be deeper than the stand to hide the seam that joins collar to neckline.

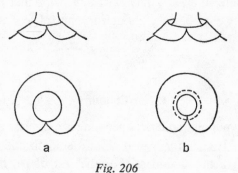

Fig. 206

Any collar which conforms to the shape and length of the neckline lies flat (Fig. 206a). This may be very little better than a collarless neckline. A collar looks prettier when there is even a small stand. To do this, shorten the neckline of the collar by ½ inch. (The broken line in Fig. 206b represents the original neckline. The solid line is the raised and shortened neckline.) As the collar is stretched to fit the neckline of the garment it is pushed into a soft roll (Fig. 206b).

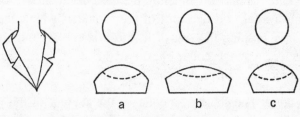

Fig. 207

When the neckline of the collar curves in the opposite direction to the curve of the bodice neckline, the short style line pushes the collar into a stand (Fig. 207a). The deeper the collar neckline curve, the higher the stand. The shallower the collar neckline curve, the lower the stand. Therefore, to lower a high stand: flatten the curve of the collar neckline. This automatically lengthens the style line (Fig. 207b). To raise a low stand: deepen the curve of the collar neckline. This automatically shortens the style line (Fig. 207c). Be sure to adjust the fall of the collar accordingly.

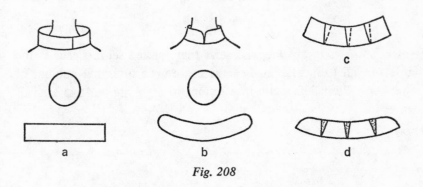

Fig. 208

The ring collar is a straight band whose neckline is the exact length of the garment neckline (Fig. 208a). Because of its straight shape, it stands away from the neck.

The mandarin collar is similarly a standing collar but it has a curved shape which makes it fit closer to the neck (Fig. 208b).

A ring collar can be changed to fit more like a mandarin collar—simply slash and overlap the pattern to the desired degree of curve (Fig. 208c).

A mandarin collar can be straightened so it stands more like a ring collar. Slash and spread the pattern to the desired degree of straightness (Fig. 208d).

It is wise not to cut out the collar in the garment fabric until the garment has been fitted, stitched, and pressed. Only then can you be sure of the exact length and shape of the neckline. Furthermore, it is also wise, first to test the fit of the collar in interfacing material even before cutting the collar in fabric. It is easier and cheaper to make changes in the interfacing. Changes up to ⅝ inch (a seam allowance) can be made on the center back of the collar pattern. If the change is more than this, make it in several places.

In testing, always *lap* the collar neck seam over the garment neck seam. This is the only way in which you can get a reasonable idea of how the collar will fit and fall.

There is no hiding a collar. It's right up there where everyone can see it. Its fit must be precise.

Sleeve Styles

It is no news to anyone who sews that a fitted set-in sleeve is the hardest of all to handle. In fact there are an astonishing number of sewers who limit their pattern selections to anything but this kind of sleeve.

THE SLEEVELESS STYLE

Fashion has been kind in recent years to the fearful sewer. She couldn't dream up anything that comes closer to her wishes than the sleeveless style.

A sleeveless dress is not just one with the sleeves left out. It has a design all its own. While a dress with sleeves needs an armscye large enough to provide ease of movement, the sleeveless dress has no such problem. Nothing hampers its movement. It can afford to be built up closer to the arm. This is the construction of the familiar sleeveless dress (Fig. 209a).

With the usual perversity of fashion, the geometric designs of the past few years have given rise to a whole new crop of sleeveless dresses so cut away as to defy all the general rules for sleeveless dresses stated above (Fig. 209b and c).

Whether your sleeveless dress is built-up or exposed depends on the beauty of this part of your anatomy. In either case, the fitting is close on the underarm—the fitting accorded all décolleté dresses.

Fig. 209

THE KIMONO SLEEVE

It is easy to understand the universal and timeless appeal of the kimono sleeve. It is easy to sew, easy to fit, and easy to wear.

An unfitted kimono sleeve is comfortable to wear and problem-

Fig. 210

free to construct (Fig. 210a). The deeper it is, the more freedom (Fig. 210b), but it has limited uses in our climate. It could hardly be worn under a coat.

There is an inevitable amount of wrinkling on the underarm of a deep kimono sleeve. This is the nature of the kimono sleeve. The looseness prevents tearing under the arm.

As a kimono sleeve becomes more fitted, the wrinkles disappear. Its freedom of movement lessens while the sewing problems increase. With the insertion of a hinge (gusset), movement is restored (Fig. 210c). The remaining problem is a neat insertion of the gusset. This causes as much anxiety for the home sewer as the setting and stitching of a fitted sleeve. The difficulty is easily overcome by hand stitching.

1. Stay stitch the gusset opening for reinforcement.
2. Carefully mark the seam line of the gusset with basting thread.
3. Turn under the seam allowance of the slashed opening. Press or baste to position.
4. Lap the folded edge of the slash over the right side of the gusset, bringing the fold to the marked seam line. Pin to position.
5. Using matching thread, slip stitch the gusset. Reinforce the corners with tiny whipping stitches.

An alternate method of reinforcement is a faced opening. This takes a little longer but repays the effort with a neat and safe finish.

1. Cut a 1½ inch wide strip of matching organza. Make it the length of the slash plus ⅝ inch.
2. Place the center of the organza strip over the slash line. Stitch in the same way one would the stay stitching.
3. Slash to the point of the stitching.
4. Turn the organza to the inside concealing the seam. Press to position.

Then proceed with steps 4 and 5 of the stay-stitched reinforcement.

A sensible rule for home sewers: when in doubt or in trouble, sew it by hand.

The same rules apply to the fitting of the shoulder of a kimono sleeve as for fitting any other shoulder. The shoulder seam line is

Fig. 211

carried down the full length of the sleeve. When properly placed, the side seam appears a continuation of this line (Fig. 211a).

A cap sleeve is a very short kimono sleeve (Fig. 211b). It is fitted in the same way.

THE RAGLAN SLEEVE

A kimono sleeve is really part of the bodice. In your pattern, you will note that the sleeve is cut all-in-one with the bodice. There are a whole group of sleeves, however, that are cut all-in-one with *part of the bodice* and retain only the underarm curve. The raglan is such a sleeve.

When a sleeve is joined with part of the bodice, it must be pinned to position before any fitting is possible. The bodice would be incomplete without it. Opportunity for fitting exists wherever there is a seam. In this case, it is the diagonal seam that joins bodice and sleeve at front and back.

When there is a shoulder seam as in Fig. 212a it is fitted like the kimono sleeve. Often in place of a seam, the shoulder is fitted by a dart (Fig. 212b). The dart must then be placed in the same position a seam would have been if there were one. This could mean moving

Fig. 212

c   d

Fig. 212

the shoulder dart forward or backward to make it really fit the shoulder. For a shapely fit the dart may be curved instead of straight.

THE STRAP OR EPAULET SLEEVE

In the strap sleeve (Fig. 212c), a section of the shoulder is attached to the top of the sleeve cap. It is possible to alter the sleeve for fit but changing the strap is tampering with the design. Should you need to make any alterations in the pattern of the sleeve, cut the strap from the sleeve, make the changes, and Scotch tape it back to position.

In fitting, center the strap on the normal shoulder line. Use the seams that join the strap to the bodice for fitting. Preserve the shape of the strap by doing any necessary fitting on the bodice.

SLEEVE-AND-YOKE IN ONE

For a sleeve-and-yoke-in-one design (Fig. 212d), follow all the rules for fitting the kimono sleeve (page 272) and for fitting a yoke (page 246).

Fitting Jackets and Coats

Everything that one can say of fitting in general and in particular can also be said of jackets and coats.

The only difference is the question of ease. Just remember that jackets and coats are worn over other garments. It is also likely that they will contain more in the way of understructure for which an ease allowance must also be made.

Fig. 213

Fig. 213

Coats are in the main easiest of all garments to fit. They hang from the shoulders and are generally unfitted (Fig. 213a) or semifitted. Even fitted coats (Fig. 213b) are not quite as fitted as dresses.

Unfitted jackets (Fig. 213c) are as easy to fit as unfitted coats. Fitted jackets require precision (Fig. 213d).

About the nicest thing you can say of a dress is that it is "tailored to fit." So special is this kind of fit that the word "tailored" has come into the language when referring to something made to a turn or adapted to suit a special need. When something is "tailored to a T" this is about the ultimate in custom-made perfection.

Fig. 213

New Styles—New Problems—New Fun

Having found a formula for clothes that fit, some women play it safe by limiting themselves to a one-style, one-shape wardrobe whatever the fashion, whatever the season. In their hands, even styles which start out adventurously are reduced to a sameness in an effort to make them fit. What a pity, when fashion is always full of excitement and new designs offer as many opportunities for flattering fit as the old ones.

Chapter IX

FIRST FLUSH TO FINAL FITTING

HOW TO MAKE AND FIT A TRIAL MUSLIN PLUS
SOME GENERAL SUGGESTIONS ON FITTING PROCEDURES

Sewers make impossible demands of themselves. Without much training and often with limited experience, they blithely go about selecting fabric and pattern. Swiftly (more or less) they cut out, stitch up, and worry about fitting at various stages in between. And, oh yes! They do expect to come up with a winner every time!

If a manufacturer or a couturier operated in this fashion, he would go out of business in no time flat. Before a design is put into production, a whole host of experts (designer, stylist, fabric and trimming people, patternmaker and draper, sample maker, illustrator, salesman, boss—even the boss's wife) may spend weeks developing and testing it.

In home sewing, the sewer herself must make all the decisions. While it is true she does not have to perfect the original design, she does have the sizable job of adapting it to her needs and her figure. Though in a smaller measure, a garment is a major investment in time and money for the home sewer as well as the manufacturer. Opportunities for change are so limited once the material is cut. Doesn't it make sense to do some experimenting in an inexpensive material before one cuts into valuable yardage?

Trying on a pinned-together paper pattern gives no idea of how a dress will fit. Pattern changes alone cannot guarantee the proper fit. It is only in fabric that one can truly make a test. This test is generally made in muslin—bleached or unbleached—of a weight and texture closest to that of the fabric. If the fabric of the garment-to-be is sheer or if the design calls for drapery, use voile, batiste, or any similar fabric for testing. If you use an inexpensive cotton you get a bonus: a dress to wear around the house when you are through. Many sewers feel they save sewing time by making the test in the lining or underlining of the garment.

Do it always? Use your judgment. If you are very sure of a particular style and certain of its fit, or if you know just how to go about making any needed changes and have sufficient material allowed for them, then a test muslin may not be necessary. If you have any doubts about whether the style is becoming to you or whether the possibilities for fitting are there, then *do* make a trial muslin.

Whatever you use for the trial, treat the test material as if it were precious fabric. It must be cut with as much thought and care as the eventual fabric. How it hangs and how it fits depend on this.

Prepare the Pattern for the Trial

For the trial, you need not cut every last little piece of pattern. The shell of the garment will do. Omit double thicknesses unless they are cut all-in-one with the pattern (facings, collars, etc.).

1. Select the pattern pieces you will need. Put the rest away in the pattern envelope.

2. Press out any wrinkles in the pattern with a warm iron.

3. Make the necessary pattern alterations.

4. Make certain that the grain line extends throughout the entire length of the pattern.

Prepare Your Own Layout Chart

Since you will not be cutting out all of the pattern and since muslin generally comes in 35-inch widths, the pattern suggestions for yardage and layout may be of very little help to you. If you buy a piece especially for this trial, you will have to approximate the necessary yardage. Many sewers who sew a great deal keep a supply on hand for use as necessary.

Devise your own layout chart. Decide which pattern sections need to be put on a fold and the kind of fold it should be—lengthwise, crosswise, partial, open single, open double, or any combination thereof. Do examine the pattern layout chart for suggestions on placement and relative position of pattern pieces. While you may not be able to duplicate the arrangement, you can benefit from the information. Since color and directional design are no problem in muslin, the pieces can be locked into position without regard for "ups" or "downs" of nap or motifs.

Place the largest pieces first, then fit in the smaller ones.

Prepare the Muslin

1. Tear the muslin at each cut end to establish the horizontal grain.

2. Fold the muslin as necessary. Pin the torn edges together. Pin the selvages together. If the material does not lie perfectly flat in this rectangular shape, dampen it and press it to position. Sometimes pulling across the bias is sufficient.

3. Test all four corners of the muslin against any right angle to make certain that the material lies in a perfect rectangle. Any of the right angle instruments referred to earlier in this book can be used. (See page 102.) Or, you can make the test against the corner of the cutting board or table.

Lay Out the Pattern and Cut

1. Follow the layout chart you have devised. Since muslin is comparatively inexpensive, don't scrounge out every last ¼ inch as you would in fine fabric. You can afford to be a little spendthrift about a few inches if it will speed the cutting.

2. Place the pattern on the muslin with the grain lines parallel to the selvages.

3. Place the pins close to the cutting edge about 2 inches apart. You may want to leave larger seam allowances to take care of unexpected changes.

4. Cut out the muslin using sharp shears or scissors.

Mark the Muslin

1. Transfer *all* pattern markings to the muslin using dressmaker's carbon paper and a tracing wheel. Use a ruler for the straight lines. Trace the curved lines freehand.

2. Mark everything—all stitching lines, seams, and darts; all △'s, ☐'s, ◯'s, the placement of buttonholes, buttons, and pockets; the point at which the collar joins the garment; any special placement or detail. *Be sure to mark the center front and the center back.* Cut out the notches. If you feel it will help with the fitting, mark the vertical and horizontal grains in colored pencil.

Optional: To get the full impact of the design, that is as full as one can in neutral muslin, sketch in the buttons in the correct size and/or any trimmings. Lightly sketch in the outlines of design units, stripes, checks, plaids. This is not a test of art ability. It is merely a matter of placement and size of units. Sketches of this kind may even help later when it comes to matching sections in your layout.

Put the Muslin Together

The quickest way to get the effect of the finished garment without actually stitching is to *lap and pin all stitching lines.* Pinning gives all the wanted information. It is much easier to unpin and repin than to rip the stitching and repin.

1. Work with the marked side up.
2. Place the pins lengthwise in a fairly continuous line along the seam to simulate stitching.
3. Take full seam allowances. If you pin too close to the cut edge you will be testing a garment at least one size larger—perhaps more, depending on the number of sections that need joining.
4. To lap the darts: slash one dart leg, lap over the other. Pin along the stitching line. Should the darts need relocation in the fitting, the slash can be repaired with Scotch tape.
5. Ease or stretch where necessary to make seam lines fit.

6. *Clip all curves,* otherwise you will be fitting on the cutting edge rather than the stitching line.

7. Lap and pin the seam line of the undercollar over the neckline seam line of the garment stretching the collar to make it fit the garment. Start at the point where collar joins garment at the front and work toward the center back. Lap the center-back seams making any necessary adjustments.

8. Make two rows of running stitches (or machine basting) across the cap of the sleeve. Pull up the gathers to form the sleeve cap. Lap the seam line of the cap over the armhole seam line. Pin.

9. Tentatively pin up all the hems to get the general effect of the garment.

Now, Try On the Muslin

This is the first of many times you will try on the garment—sometimes to make a judgment and sometimes merely to admire your handiwork. The impulse is irresistible. Just remember that this is muslin; it cannot possibly be as flattering as it will eventually be in your lovely fabric. Remember, too, that the effect will be different when the supporting interfacing or underlining is added and the garment is pressed and blocked to shape.

Bring the trial muslin as close to perfection as you can knowing that there will yet be many refinements as the work progresses.

Just what is it that we are looking for in the muslin? The answers to these questions: Is the style good? Is the size right? Does it fit well? What needs doing?

IS THE STYLE GOOD?

If you were buying a dress, you might very well try on a dozen or more in as many different shops before you found one that was just right for you. The muslin trial is the sewer's equivalent of that trying-on jaunt. Those beautiful photographs and alluring sketches may look great in the pattern books and on the pattern envelopes but on you—? Better know *now* if that style does anything for you—now—before the frustrations of trying to salvage an unsalvageable problem.

Many a sewer has been known to abandon a pattern upon seeing the muslin and finding how impossible it is to make it fit with even a modest degree of flattery. Many find that a few changes in the muslin may vastly improve the becomingness of a style.

IS THE SIZE RIGHT?

Is there too much fullness for you or too little? Would this be a question of style or one of size? Perhaps a smaller or larger pattern in the same style would be the answer. Perhaps a little more or less ease would do the trick.

DOES IT FIT WELL?

If the style and the size are right, your next consideration is how the muslin fits. How you handle this is the summation of all you have learned thus far on fitting. Reread Chapters V and VI to refresh your memory. Many of the directions for fitting the muslin basic pattern (page 161) are applicable to this trial muslin.

Some General Suggestions Regarding Fitting

Fitting is fitting whether it is in muslin or in your chosen fabric. All the elements that constitute good fit are the same for both. The following considerations are valid for both!

Familiarize yourself with current styles. Chic in this year's look may be a subtle change of line and proportion—a mere pinch here or there. Read the news reports and the fashion magazines. Look in the shops. Observe well-dressed women. Train your eye to see small niceties.

Make mental calculations as to how to achieve an effect. This can be a great game. No woman will be safe from your analytic gaze. That's fine. It's these clinical observations of that gal sitting in front of you in church or across from you on the bus that may teach you what not to do as well as what to do. As your perception grows, you'll grow more demanding about fit until you reach the point of ultimate perfection.

Be fastidious but not hypercritical of your fitting. Many a sewer worries herself through every last ⅛ inch. There is nothing quite like the zeal of the newly converted in whatever it is they were recently converted to. This goes for those who have just discovered the art of fitting. There is a point at which you can get too much of a good thing. Quit while you're ahead. They do say it takes two to paint a picture: one to do the painting, the other to clobber him when the painting (rather than he) is finished. The same could be said for fitting.

Pace yourself. Work quickly with materials that ravel—like raw silk. Take your time with stretchy fabrics. Give them time to stabilize themselves before the final fitting.

When fitting or being fitted stand in a natural position. Clothes must fit your posture as well as your measurements. If you "stand up straight" or "pull your shoulders back" or "tuck your stomach in" for a fitting (frequent admonitions), the garment may not fit you when you are at ease and in your normal posture. If your posture is bad, do something about it for its own sake. Don't indulge in temporary gymnastics at the expense of your fitting.

Allow sufficient ease to be comfortable. Remember that more fabrics won't give than will.

Don't overfit! Contrary to popular notion, tight fitting is not slimming. It outlines the figure and focuses attention on all one's figure faults.

If you fit yourself, use safety pins rather than straight pins for strategic marking. They won't fall out as you maneuver your fitting and remove the garment.

All fitting is done from the right side. Corrections are transferred to the wrong side for stitching. Were you to do your fitting inside out you would be fitting the opposite side of you—inside right becomes outside left, inside left becomes outside right. If you fit in reverse, you defeat the whole purpose of fitting.

Pin the garment closed on the correct line. This is fixed by the design and you must not take liberties with it. There are too many style details dependent on the closing—extensions, collar, lapel, neckline, facings, even the position of the darts. While it may be tempting to give oneself a little more ease on this line or to make a double-breasted lap of a single-breasted garment, the pattern changes involved are too difficult for anyone unacquainted with patternmaking.

When a pattern calls for a stay to control the fullness of a design, fit the stay before adding the fullness. It is the relation of the stay to the figure that produces the actual fit of the garment. The fullness or drapery is just so much decoration held in place by the stay.

Pin all slits and pleats closed. The garment should fit without relying on their released fullness for added width.

Tentatively pin up the hems of skirt and sleeve. You will get a much better idea of how to fit in proportion to the length.

Examine the fit. If changes need to be made, start at the shoulders and work down checking the grain, ease, dart control, silhouette seams. Starting at the neckline and working down, check the style features of neckline, collar, sleeves, etc. Locate the position of buttons and buttonholes. Locate the position of applied pockets and trimmings.

Muslin to Pattern

When the muslin has been fitted to your satisfaction, any alterations made on it must be transferred to the pattern. It is the pattern which is used for layout, cutting, and marking, not the muslin. Muslin has been known to stretch, ripple, wrinkle. Furthermore, it can easily be coaxed into incorrect shape in order to lock the layout in a forced arrangement. The paper pattern is an accurate and incorruptible record.

1. Mark all changes on the muslin in colored pen or pencil. The marks are placed along the pin lines of the fitting. (Correct any "jumpiness" of the pins.) The pin line is the new seam line.

2. When marked, unpin the muslin completely. Flatten each piece. Press, if necessary.

3. Pin the paper pattern on the muslin matching at key points. The corrections being in color should be clearly visible through the tissue.

4. Trace the corrections directly on the pattern. Use colored pen or pencil so there will be no mistaking the new line.

5. Complete the pattern in any way necessary, to record *all*

changes. You should be able to follow the pattern without wondering whether you did or didn't and just how much.

6. Make sure that all corresponding seams match in length, that each pair of dart legs is of equal length, that all facings or joining sections have been altered to match.

7. When the position of a dart has been changed, make certain that you have included enough material at its end to be caught into the seam.

8. True up all stitching lines with the drafting instruments.

9. Use the corrected pattern for the layout and cutting.

10. Be sure to make corresponding pattern changes on interfacings, linings, underlinings, and interlinings.

Organize the Sewing Sequence to Include the Fitting

Most home sewers follow (indeed, depend on) the printed directions in the pattern for putting the garment together. These *pattern directions deal with construction not fitting.* That is left to the sewer. No pattern company could possibly anticipate or have room for a consideration of all the individual fitting problems involved.

From the standpoint of fitting, the suggested step-by-step sewing directions may not be a logical or satisfactory order of work for some individuals. The sewer must then reorganize the sewing sequence to include her fittings as they are needed.

1. Stitch and press each unit of the outer and supporting fabrics following the pattern directions for construction as far as possible before a try-on. Join what seems reasonable or essential for a fitting.

2. Do as much fitting as you feel fruitful at one time. When you are satisfied that you have gone as far as you can with a fitting, remove the garment carefully. Transfer any right-side corrections to the wrong side for stitching. (Use basting thread or tailor's chalk.)

3. Do as much of the sewing as possible between fittings to make the garment ready for the next examination. Always check the stitching lines from the right side. Correct any wavy lines or bulges with slip basting. Restitch on the wrong side.

Everyone who sews develops a style of working that suits her temperament. Even when the home sewer is working against a time deadline she is still not under the same pressures as if she were sewing for her living. She can afford to be a little more generous with her time and her fittings. She can suit the number and kind of fittings to her needs and her pace. Admittedly this would be highly unprofitable for a commercial venture but it is highly profitable for the home sewer.

The Final (?) Fitting

How many times should a garment be fitted? As many times as it takes to make it fit. This varies with the experience of the fitter, the complexity of the design, and the waywardness of the figure.

Some mail order houses make clothes by measurements alone—no fitting at all. This method produces highly questionable results. Some dressmakers make a dress with only one fitting. Some take two, some many more. Many custom houses use their clients' dressmaker's dummys to spare them the hours of standing for a fitting.

Why is all the fitting necessary when one has already gone to such lengths to guarantee good fit? Measurements, a basic pattern, pattern alterations, a dress form, a trial muslin—all are extremely helpful. Yet, in the end, nothing can take the place of fitting the garment fabric on the person.

Each fabric has its own unique qualities. Muslin can tell you some things about how your garment will fit. Only the cloth of your garment can exploit the illusions created with color and texture.

Fitting is not just a question of measurements or even of shaping. It is how all the elements in combination make for a dress, a gown, a suit, a coat that looks good, feels comfortable on, and is as lovely in motion as in standing still. The preliminaries bring us within sight of excellent fit. It is the garment itself that is the final trial.

Hopefully, there is a final fitting—though this may not be when you think you have finished. Often after a first wearing you may decide some small changes are necessary. This is a common experience. If you are a perfectionist this refining and polishing will go on until you get that cherished project to fit precisely as you desire it.

Anguished Search to Fond Fulfillment

Fitting is the culmination of all one can learn of design, of fabrics, of patterns, of construction. Perfection is achieved only when all work together in harmony. This is something that the creators of fashion know full well. Home sewers who aspire to a professional look for their clothes must know this equally well. There are not two sets of rules and standards. If a dress is to be beautiful the same considerations must go into the making of it be the creator professional or non-professional.

It wasn't always hard. A fig leaf didn't take much doing. Drapery was a cinch. The chemise was simple, the tunic, terrific. Sometime along about the middle of the eleventh century some daring Gothic beauty shed her shift and donned a gown that left no doubt about the lines of her figure. That was our undoing.

What may have been a medieval lark became a millennium-long headache: how to achieve that delicate balance between the lines of the design and the lines of the figure that is the essence of flattering fit.

If we persist in wearing clothes sculptured to reveal our natural charms, that anguished search for perfect fit may well last another thousand years. Unless we all become quite learned and adept at How TO MAKE CLOTHES THAT FIT AND FLATTER—which seems a fitting thought with which to close this book.

INDEX